"This book is a larger-than-life love letter to the music and people and culture of NYC that will flip everything you know about the seedy nightclub business to prove the safest space and brightest light can often be found in the darkest places—with the nicest people.

Club owner Lon Ballinger miraculously pulled off Webster Hall's "Greatest Show on Earth" for more than two decades with his merry band of brothers, the unique spirit of a do-no-evil hustler, and a battle-axe mother who never let the city's biggest party distract her from counting every sweat-soaked dollar."

SMOKEY FONTAINE
Editor-in-Chief, Apple

PARTY BOYS

HOW THE BALLINGER BROTHERS BUILT THE BEST NIGHTCLUBS IN THE WORLD

Lon Ballinger

PARTY BOYS: How the Ballinger Brothers
Built the Best Nightclubs in the World
Copyright © 2024 Lon Ballinger

PartyBoysNewYork.com
Mount Kisco, New York

First Edition
ISBN: 979-8-9902153-0-6 (paperback)

Produced in the United States of America

Cover and interior design: Lee Silber
Photo collages: Lee Silber
Cover and interior layout and typesetting: Andrew Chapman
Editing: Tammy Ditmore

CONTENTS

This book is dedicated to my wife, Lois.
And thank you to my family and the millions of people
we got to share our nightclubs with. Thank you all!

PREFACE

PARTY BOYS is my memoir of real nightlife experiences and how I stood on the dance floors, behind the bars and stages, in the green rooms, or snuggled away in some other little hole in one of our famous nightclubs for over 40 years. It was from this front-row seat and behind-the-scenes vantage point I watched as music and society morphed and changed consistently and dramatically—sometimes for the better, sometimes not. I have done my best to be truthful and relevant about nightlife, nightclubs, and night people—particularly from 1977 to 2017. I believe you will not only be captivated by this collection of compelling stories, but you will also learn some valuable lessons about business, human behavior, and music history.

Lon Ballinger
Hudson Valley, New York
February, 2024

"I always told my family and friends that I had the best job in the world. Imagine the luxury of telling your wife and kids, 'I'm going to work now. We got 3,000 people waiting to have fun and dance tonight.' So I always went to work thinking I was the luckiest man on earth."

MEET THE PARTY BOYS

My brothers and I created nightclubs that felt like antique farmhouses with magic spells cast upon them. Maze-like passageways led to dance floors pulsing with music and mesmerizing lights. Go-go dancers cast their shadows across the walls, inviting clubgoers to join them in a night of carefree fun. In forty years of business, we drew more than 40 million people to our clubs to dance and listen to music, to gather with old friends and meet new ones.

We became known as the Party Boys courtesy of the Toronto media, mainly because we knew how to throw a party and attract a lot of people to our parties. Very early in our careers, we realized we could create great opportunities for ourselves in a changing nightlife landscape. We recognized that we could help shape a booming new nightclub era and make a lot of money all while having a lot of fun—if we did it right. And we did—together.

In many ways my brothers and I had a lot in common, including our values and our drive—in addition to our parents and growing-up years, of course. But man, in other ways, you could not find four more different people to form a partnership. And that's probably why it worked so well. There were five of us, including my sister, and we managed to work together for decades because we all respected the unique talents and strengths that each one of us brought to our partnership. Let me introduce you to my family, the Ballingers.

GAIL "THE ELDER" BALLINGER LOVE

The unsung hero of our story is our older sister, Gail, who was born in 1946. The only girl in the bunch, Gail supported us for many years by driving us around, feeding us, and loving us. She even picked the pizza parlor that put her brothers on the road to success.

STEPHEN (STEVE) BALLINGER

Without Steve's brave and intrepid spirit, none of our success would have been possible. Born in 1949, Steve was a true visionary who combined his creativity with confidence, ambition, and determination. His go-for-broke attitude carried us through many challenges.

LORNE (LON) BALLINGER

Born in 1950, I was the middle child who would probably be best described as the "leader" of the group. I was also the real estate and marketing expert who helped facilitate the purchase and sales of our many properties and projects and pioneered radio marketing techniques for our nightclubs. I was probably the most involved in Webster Hall on a daily basis and visible to the staff and public over the years.

PETER BALLINGER

Peter, born in 1952, is likely the smartest Ballinger of all. He was excellent at making sure anything that needed to get done got done right— and on time. He was the least likely to rock the boat and was supportive of all our wild and crazy ideas. But he never joined us on a regular basis in New York City; instead, he bought a garlic farm and lived a gentlemen farmer's life while creating a multimillion-dollar farming empire.

PATRICK BALLINGER

Patrick was born in 1954 but died in infancy.

"BUSTER" BALLINGER

The baby of the family, Buster was born in 1956. A design genius and a truly unique artist, he applied his creativity to every project we attempted. When it came to making a property unique and successful, no one was better than Buster.

"When you combine the right music, in the right place, at the right time—and add in a few gimmicks, a lot of fun, and running things the right way—you have our recipe for success."

NICE GUYS DON'T ALWAYS FINISH LAST

During the days of the Party Boys, Webster Hall, New York, packed its four floors with multiple stage cultures and a variety of music and dance styles and experiences. There was something for everyone. This book is built the same way; it's like four books in one.

Interested in celebrities? Find out what some of the biggest names in music were really like behind the scenes.

Looking for sound career and business advice? My brothers and I achieved great success while also learning some painful lessons along the way. Let someone who has been there and done that share some behind-the-velvet-rope insights and errors so you can avoid making the same mistakes we did.

Ever wonder what it's like to own one of the greatest nightclubs in the free world? My stories from a lifetime in the entertainment industry may surprise and shock you.

Need some inspiration and motivation? Learn how five dirt-poor, farm kids from a small rural community in Canada overcame a multitude of obstacles to create an entertainment empire and run the most influential nightclub in New York City, of all places. Despite our early challenges—or maybe because of them—my family beat the odds. We made the most of what we had, took a lot of chances, got some lucky breaks, worked together, and learned how to always finish strong.

We achieved success in a cutthroat industry in a city known for devouring its own while overseeing four floors of performers and tending a business filled with thousands of people partying on a nightly basis. And we did it while striving to always treat everyone—from the custodian to the superstar—with respect, dignity, and compassion. Hopefully, our legacy demonstrates that nice guys can finish first and that doing the right thing is always the right thing to do.

The Ballinger Brothers witnessed—and made—some history during the decades we operated our clubs in Canada and at Webster Hall. From my front-row seat to the music and entertainment industry, I witnessed the birth of music videos, hip-hop, EDM, and digital products and the death of albums and CDs and other elements of the analog music industry.

The Party Boys tells the story of how we came to the entertainment industry as rank novices and left as the best nightclub operators in the world. And learned valuable lessons while sharing our lives with the nearly 40 million people who turned up in our clubs over our forty-year career.

Read on to be educated, enlightened, and entertained by the story behind the success of the Ballingers and their journey from a corner pizza shop in a tiny Canadian town to Webster Hall, the greatest nightclub in the entertainment capital of the world.

GROWING UP ON THE FAMILY FARM

CHAPTER 1

THE "FRUITS" OF OUR LABOR

As kids growing up in the 1950s and 1960s, we were dirt poor, but we didn't really know how little we had, partly because no one had much in rural northern Canada in those days. We weren't embarrassed by our poverty, and growing up with a nothing-to-lose and nothing-to-fall-back-on mentality served us well then and later in life.

When I look back on our sibling success, I think it might have started in the late summer months of 1956. Our parents had moved us a few years earlier from Montreal to a farm near Dundalk, Ontario, thinking it would be a good place to raise their kids. When my siblings and I discovered a dilapidated orchard at the back of the farm, we collected enough apples to fill a few baskets and set up a little stand in front of our house, intent on earning a few bucks.

We must have been a sight to see. Four skinny, dust-covered kids, ranging in age from four to ten, in hand-me-down clothes, holding up ratty handwritten signs hawking wormy apples from our run-down farm. Sometimes we had our baby brother, Buster, with us too.

Only we didn't see ourselves as ratty-looking kids. We were just four enthusiastic salesmen, eagerly awaiting our next potential customer, confident we could make a deal with anyone who would stop. Not many cars actually traveled the side road that ran in front of our farm, but we waited patiently, looking for clouds of dust in the distance and straining our ears for the growl of an engine that would signal another sales opportunity.

When a car or truck (or occasional tractor) approached, we would hop up and down and wave wildly, hoping beyond hope that any driver who stopped would be ready to give us a quarter in exchange for one of our old baskets of apples. Looking back now, I'm sure the drivers who did stop and buy our wares were motivated more by sympathy for these little ragamuffins than by their desire for apples. But we didn't know that then—and it would not have mattered if we did. A sale was a sale.

By the end of the summer we sold out of everything we had—roughly two dozen baskets full of produce. We gave the small fortune we made—around fifteen dollars—to our mom to help pay an outstanding bill she had been fretting over.

Our little apple stand provided us with our first and best business lessons. It demonstrated how our willingness to think creatively and work enthusiastically could overcome a lot of obstacles—including an out-of-the-way location. And knowing that people wanted to buy apples we had hand-picked, polished, and packaged gave us a sense of pride in our work.

A few years later, my brothers and I proved that our flair for sales extended beyond wormy apples when we dominated the sales of raffle tickets for a school fund-raiser. Going door to door, we raised $125 selling tickets for ten cents each or three for a quarter. The rest of the kids in our one-room school didn't even manage to sell $10 worth of tickets. The raffle winner got a hockey sweater while the funds from ticket sales helped provide holiday food for families and a school trip to Niagara Falls.

And the Ballinger family got a lesson in what we could do when we all pulled together.

CHAPTER 2

THE SCHOOL OF HARD KNOCKS

"You smashed his skull!"

I was trying not to panic, but my brother Stephen was gasping for air, moaning and writhing on the cold concrete floor in the basement of the one-room schoolhouse. A tall gangly farm boy stood above him, holding a baseball bat while another kid screamed for our school's teacher.

"Hurry, Mrs. Chisholm, please. Steve Ballinger is dying!"

The teacher rushed in and immediately told another student to run to the farmhouse next door and call my mother. The call went out on the neighborhood "party line," so word quickly spread that Steve Ballinger had been rushed to the hospital with a fractured skull.

Steve pulled through, but he required weeks of care and rehab. And our family was forced to face the realities of life in the rural community where we had moved after my dad had wrapped up his military service in Montreal. There was no legal retribution for the teenage farm boys who had beaten Steve within an inch of his life. They had attacked him simply because we were new to the area and they thought we might be different.

In our early days on the farm, bullies would often knock our hats off our heads when we went to town for groceries or supplies. Or they would hit us with hockey sticks if they managed to catch us alone. When my mother found nine-year-old Peter bruised and crying after a big kid had smacked him silly outside the Dundalk hockey rink, she determined that we were going to teach bully boys a lesson about tormenting the Ballinger Brothers.

She gathered us together and told us in no uncertain terms we had to teach this particular bully a lesson because there was no one else who was going to protect us. Soon, we devised a plan that we would remember whenever we had to deal with aggressive troublemakers for the rest of our lives.

A week or so after Peter had been beaten up, Stephen and I hid behind a huge snowbank near the home of the bully, who was about fifteen. Steve was twelve and I was 11 at the time, but we waited eagerly for him to return home, hockey sticks in hand.

When he sauntered by, we jumped out, ready for revenge even though we were half the bully's size. Smacking him with our junior-sized hockey sticks, we yelled, "Never hit our brother, or any of us ever again, or you'll get it worse next time."

Whimpering and cowering on the ground, the bully begged us to stop and promised us he would never again target a Ballinger brother. When we heard his promise, we backed off and watched as he ran down the street to his fancy home, crying all the way.

Word slowly spread that if you messed with one of the Ballingers, you messed with all of them. The bullies didn't bother us too much after that.

Early in life, my brothers and I learned from the school of hard knocks that you should not go looking for trouble, but you should never back down from it, either. Our mother's plan showed us that most bullies are babies when you confront them head-on and forcefully and that letting problems linger only causes bigger problems down the road.

That was just one of the many, many lessons we learned from our mother.

"If you don't have anything positive to say, then say nothing at all—unless you were our mom, then all bets were off. "

CHAPTER 3

THE INCOMPARABLE MRS. B

Some people are simply larger than life. My mother, Eleanor Jean, was one of those people. When we were kids, our mother was not only physically imposing, but her temper and erratic behavior made her downright frightening.

Whenever any one of us made her angry—which was very easy to do—she would line us up and whip each of us with a piece of rubber cut from a mud flap of an old truck. We didn't dare argue with her or plead our case because we knew there was no reason to expect her to act rationally at that point. We also didn't dare skip the punishment line because we would get it twice as bad when she caught up with us.

Mom reveled in her power, often pitting one brother against another to try to get her way. She terrified us all one day in 1960 when she grabbed Buster and held a knife to his throat, threatening him because we older kids had done something to upset her. "I'll kill him . . . I'll kill him," she screamed. All of us worried that she just might do it. But looking back on the situation now, I realize it was just part of her drama queen shtick.

Mom feared no man, and she liked no woman. She seldom had a kind word for anyone but possessed a vast capacity to be mean and critical. She was especially harsh with women she thought were weak and whiny. While Mom loved big handsome men, she would even target them when she was in the grips of her darkness.

However, despite the harsh words and biting criticism, the accusations, manipulations, and unexpected outbursts, we knew Mom loved her kids fiercely. And we loved her back just as much.

My siblings and I would spend our entire lives trying to please Mom, not realizing until much later that she was a textbook narcissist with a need for constant attention and adulation and an uncanny ability to deflect fault and blame others. She always believed she was right with absolute certainty, even when she was absolutely wrong.

And yet . . .

In all honesty, I have to declare that the Ballingers would never have achieved what we did without Mom's incredible and inspiring force. She taught us to work hard and how to use our underdog status as a weapon rather than a barrier. She taught us to always believe that we could do anything we put our minds to. Most of all, she taught us fearlessness. We learned to never take shit from anyone and to be ready to fight for what was right.

But Mom also insisted that we should show respect to others and wait our turn. "Don't take the last sandwich on the plate because someone else might be hungry too," she would say.

Maybe the most valuable lesson I learned from Mom was how to keep my composure and not take it personally when other people get angry. I learned early on that when someone is raging mad, their anger isn't about me, it's about them.

When the Ballinger brothers began building their string of successful nightclubs, "Mrs. B" became a fixture at the front door. In some respects, she became the official keeper of the gate. She worked at Webster Hall for more than twenty years, showing up early in the evening and staying until the last hour. Then a security guard would escort her across the street to the apartment we rented for her.

Her nightly presence helped us create a family vibe that was a huge part of the club's family-style culture, which was one of the main reasons for our long-term success. But that doesn't mean Mom made everything easier. Mrs. B never had an unspoken thought—and more often than not, the thought wasn't nice. We frequently found ourselves doing damage control—apologizing to someone for something Mom said or did or finding an employee she had just fired and telling them to go back to work. "Mom's having a bad day today," we would explain.

Despite her orneriness, our patrons loved her, just like her kids did. Mrs. B, for all her zany and incorrigible ways, was a true character. No matter how tough or mean she appeared, her wit and humor would eventually shine through. Once, she got very sick and needed to be rushed to the hospital. I arrived just in time to see her old body strapped into the gurney for an ambulance ride.

"Mom, what's wrong?"

Without missing a beat, she looked up and said, "I'm having a baby."

Mom lived to be ninety-five, and she credited the nightclub life for keeping her going so long and helping her mind to stay sharp. When she was quite old and nearly worn out, I tried to hire caregivers to come into her home and provide help. But every time a caregiver arrived, Mom would promptly fire them.

Frustrated, I finally asked, "Mom, did I ever do anything in my life that made you happy?"

She stopped and thought for a few seconds. "Well, you never complained."

This may have been the best compliment I ever got from her—or anyone, for that matter.

Although my mom never supplied much in the way of positive reinforcement, she provided lessons and words that have helped me build a successful life, and I honor her legacy by passing those lessons on to others.

"Work hard. Don't take no for an answer. Never say you can't do something because you can. Teach yourself not to take criticism personally, because most of the time it's not about you ... it's about them."

*"I know Dad was proud of us. He was
impressed with our energy and hustle—a
hustle that I think happened because of our
desperation to escape the poverty and angst
he had helped to manifest so well for us."*

CHAPTER 4

WE KNOW HE LOVED US

It was cold, and we were tired and hungry as the sun went down on another long day of working in the fields. Then Dad told us we couldn't go inside until we fixed the combine. Frustrated and disappointed, we wondered how we would manage that. We were just kids—how were we gonna fix this piece of farm equipment?

That's when my dad said something that has stuck with me ever since.

"Man made it. Man can fix it."

That sentiment has inspired me all my life, and many people have heard me say it time and again.

That was just one of many lessons I learned from my dad. Unfortunately, most of the lessons were not so inspiring. They say we either become our parents or we become the opposite of our parents. I always tried my best to become the latter. My Dad, Lorne Ballinger, was handsome and physically strong. He feared no man and he obviously passed that attitude onto his children. He bought us boxing gloves when we were kids and taught us how to defend ourselves. He also put watermelons in our little watermelon patch to make us think we had grown them ourselves. Later, when we were building our business, he was there for us and helped in any way he could.

Sadly, I never knew the person my dad had been before he went off to war. I did see flashes of a personable, charismatic, and happy man from time to time. But the man I saw most often was the broken one who had returned from serving in the Canadian Air Force during World War II seething with anger and addicted to booze.

I know my father hated the war and all the damage it did. He had lost all his high school friends overseas in a conflict he took part in only because he knew it was his civic duty. Later in life, he became a big fan of Muhammad Ali for his stance against the Vietnam War.

My parents married in 1944, ten days after Dad returned from four-and-a-half years overseas. My high-strung mother only aggravated Dad's PTSD, as neither she nor anyone else ever seemed to understand what he had seen and experienced. They couldn't understand why he could not just go back to his normal life and old self. But the war for him was a lifelong nightmare.

For many years, Dad would leave our run-down farm every Monday morning to head for his job in the "big city." Returning late on Saturday afternoons, he would drink all day Sunday before leaving again early on Monday morning.

My parents fought over everything—especially his drinking and our family's financial woes. Living as we did with such emotionally volatile parents, our lives as children revolved around work and terror, with a few threads of happiness stitched through.

But our crazy home life actually turned out to be a kind of a benefit for my brothers and me later in life when we had to deal with difficult people, strong personalities, and bad behavior due to addiction or other issues. We had seen it all before.

Unfortunately, some of the things we saw and lived through influenced who we were as kids—and adults. My parents would fight tooth and nail and say the nastiest things to each other. Sometimes my siblings did the same—fighting with each other just like we had watched our parents fight. My father was a raging alcoholic, and although I quit drinking later in life, alcohol was an issue for all of us at one time or another.

When I was thirteen, Dad finally moved out officially, away from his kids and his distant, demanding, harsh wife. He lived by himself and drove trucks in Toronto. Dad tried returning to the family years later, but sadly, by then he was almost irrelevant to us. We had learned to get by on our own, and we all knew we could never count on our father.

Dad did live long enough to see his sons' success, and I think he was proud of all we accomplished—although he never said much about it. But he did once tell me that his own dad would have been very proud of us.

Another time he told me he loved me—but not before I had expressed my love for him. I vowed to myself that I would always tell my kids I loved them and was proud of them. And I did.

When I look back and think about my dad—as I often do—I try to remember the good times. I think about the little chocolate bars he would bring for us every Saturday night when he returned from the city. And I remember how he put little rabbit turds outside the door of our house on Easter to help convince us it was the Easter Bunny who had left a trail of tasty eggs around the old farmhouse.

My dad came up short in many basic ways, but I know deep down he loved us and was proud of us. I just wish he could have found more ways to say the words his kids so badly wanted to hear.

"In our home, complaints were never tolerated and sickness was not allowed."

CHAPTER 5

FISH AND CHIPS

I think one of the best ways to describe how poor we were as kids is to tell you that every summer my brothers and I would cut the front part off our worn-out rubber boots to allow our grimy toes a chance for some fresh air. We would also wear the same pair of threadbare shorts and nothing else—no shirts or underwear—all summer long.

Our farm was a mile from Corbetton, a desperate little village in Ontario, and five miles from Dundalk, which was way smaller than it seemed when we were kids. Located far from any metropolis, the biggest industry in Dundalk was a junkyard full of rusting cars and rotting tractors.

The family farm was built on a low-lying, flat piece of forgotten farm land in a township coined "Floatin' Proton" because it was so swampy. It came with an old gray barn, a chicken coop, a shed to store farm equipment, and a bunch of broken fences we needed to mend constantly to keep the cattle in. Our nearest neighbors (who weren't all that near) lived on similar ramshackle farms maintained by similar sad and tired families who were also hanging on by a thread.

It was a full-time job to grow hay and grain during the summer while doing our best to care for the farm animals my mom bought on the cheap at the local auction. From an early age, we were expected to know how to operate and maintain our old tractors, plows, cultivators, seed drills, and combines.

The goal was to harvest enough hay in the summer to feed the animals through the long, brutal winter. We were trying to keep alive a barn full of chickens, pigs, cattle, and even a horse. Our creatures were mostly misfits—sick or malnourished animals other farmers sold at the local auctions because there was something wrong with them.

On Sunday nights we would all get cleaned up, sharing one tub of bath water because the water heater in our basement was so tiny and slow that it would have taken all night to refill the tub for each of us. Monday mornings we would head out for the one-room schoolhouse, a mile and a half away.

On the rare day or evening when we had some spare time, my brothers and I would walk up and down the dirt roads of our township, collecting the pop and beer bottles the local lads tossed out on their many booze cruises. This was how we passed our leisure time—if such a word even existed in our young lives. It was also how we earned a buck or two.

When we collected enough dirty bottles from the low-lying ditches, Mom would take us into town to redeem them for two pennies each. We saved those pennies until we could afford to take the one big outing we dreamed about all summer: dinner and a movie.

Mom would pile us kids into our battered pickup truck and drive thirty miles to the "big" town to enjoy a feast at the fish-and-chips restaurant and the latest Western flick at the local cinema. All six of us would squeeze into the front seat of that 1957 Chevy, which was held together in places with binder twine and hay baling wire. Buster would sit on Gail's lap, while Stephen, Peter, and I would squeeze into the rest of the front seat beside Mom.

It was the highlight of our summer.

We learned early by way of severe corporal punishment to behave and do exactly what we were told when we were out in public (and at home, too). So no matter how hungry we were, all of us waited quietly and patiently for the magnificent morsels of battered fish and crispy hand-cut fries to arrive at our table. And none of us dared complain about the movie.

After our big night on the town, we would ride home in the darkness, basking in the success of a job well done and a reward well spent until we fell asleep in a heap like a litter of puppies.

When we grew up, my siblings and I continued to lean on each other as we operated our businesses and celebrated our wins—big and small—together. But few of our celebrations would ever compare to those fish-and-chip dinners.

"Keep an open mind with people and give everyone a chance to show what they can do."

CHAPTER 6

ONE TEACHER, EIGHT GRADES, IN A ONE-ROOM SCHOOLHOUSE

School was never a priority in our family. It was treated as more of a nuisance, somewhere you went to learn the basics of reading, writing, and arithmetic—and how to spell your name, if you got lucky. The important stuff was learning how to operate our farm equipment and take care of our animals.

My mother—probably because of dyslexia—only made it to the fifth grade. My father came to the party with an eighth-grade education, having gone to work for his own father before he died young as a result of World War I injuries. All my parents really knew how to do was to work hard at poor-paying jobs that required little education.

My siblings and I all struggled in school. My mother's violent mood swings always kept us on edge, and my father's absence meant that the farm work fell on us. It's surely no surprise that our schoolwork (and our grades) suffered. We were ashamed of what was happening at home, but we never discussed these matters and never asked for help. Over the years I have learned that it's not a sign of weakness to reach out for help, it's a sign of strength. But I didn't know it then.

I also didn't know why I struggled so hard to read and write. Years later, as an adult, I was diagnosed with dyslexia, and it became clear why school had been so difficult for me.

From age six to fourteen, I attended a one-room schoolhouse in the flat country among the farms. In my first year of school, there were six kids in my grade—four boys and two girls. By the end of the year, both girls were gone—one moved and one flunked out.

Mrs. Pattison, a farmer's-wife-turned-teacher, was my only teacher from first through fourth grade. Although I always tried to not make Mrs. Pattison mad, I did not always succeed. Her temper was as volatile as my parents' temper, and my school environment was as toxic as my home environment.

One day my brother Steve was struggling to spell the word "baby." He simply couldn't get it right, and Mrs. Pattison screamed at him, "Are you stupid?"

I wish now that I had been brave enough to stand up for my brother, but it was my classmate Wayne Livingston who said, "No, you're stupid!"

Our teacher yelled, "Who said that?"

The classroom went silent. We were all frozen in fear of what Mrs. Pattison would do next. Helen Marshall put up her hand and said, "Please, Mrs. Pattison, Wayne Livingston said it."

"Sit down, Helen, I know who said it," Mrs. Pattison said, her face scrunched in anger.

Without warning, she hurled a book at Wayne, striking him in the head right above his eye. Blood spilled everywhere as Mrs. Pattison grabbed Wayne's arm and dragged him to the teacher's room where she pulled out a thick leather belt and proceeded to hit him for what seemed like hours. That was my school world.

But although I can never endorse her methods, I can give Mrs. Pattison credit for helping me master math. I learned because I was so scared she would get mad at me if I didn't. Becoming good with numbers played a big role in my business success later in life.

And our nontraditional education played a role in my family's success too. Although we struggled in the classroom, my brothers and I were well schooled in life skills and challenges. To this day I believe that we got a four-year jump on our book-smart peers who went on to get college degrees.

Pooling our talents and our resources we learned how to create a business from the ground up and banked hundreds of thousands of dollars by the time we were in our mid-twenties. Although learning is the most important thing a person can do, some of your most valuable lessons might come from a farm or your dinner table or a summer job. Not everyone is designed or destined to get a college degree.

"The people who get hard things done are the people who don't know that they can't be done."

CHAPTER 7

FINDING A CHRISTMAS TREE IN THE SWAMP

Everything about life on the farm was hard. We had little money and a lot of work. We were constantly shoveling manure, mowing hay, harvesting grain, fixing fences, planting crops, and feeding animals. We did most of this backbreaking work manually or using shabby, second- or third-hand farm equipment, which left little time for activities away from the farm.

Not that we could get far from the farm anyway. We lived on an isolated plot of land in a place where winters were so harsh that we could be snowbound for days in our one snowplow town. We didn't have many childhood friends. My brothers and I had each other, but Gail was really alone.

To get things done, we had to pull together, and we had to be resourceful if we wanted anything out of the ordinary. That's why we went looking for a Christmas tree one year in the wild, sprawling swamp and vast untamed forest a few miles from our house.

We drove our beat-up pickup truck and parked it on the side of a dirt road, grabbed a handsaw and axe, and trudged off to find a Christmas tree for the family. How difficult could it be to find the perfect tree, cut it down, and drag it back? Dumb question.

The swamp was dense with thick foliage, wild bushes, and plants. There was no easy way to find the ideal Christmas tree, and we wound up walking until we were lost. It was December, the sun disappeared early, and the weather quickly went from cold to freezing cold. We didn't panic, but we were really worried about finding our way back to the road before it got fully dark.

Peter, the smallest among us, climbed the tallest tree to look for the truck, road, or any familiar landmark.

"What do you see?" we yelled up to him.

"Nothing," he called down.

"What do you mean, nothing?" I glanced at my brothers and saw fear in their eyes.

"I don't see the road or the truck is what I mean," Peter said, making his way down to the ground.

We huddled in silence, trying to come up with our next move. In those brief moments of quiet, we heard the low rumble of an old truck in the distance. Together, we gauged where the sound had come from and made our way in that direction.

We pulled each other along through the dense, dark underbrush for what seemed like hours but was likely about ten minutes. Just as the darkness rolled in, we found the road and our pickup truck.

We huddled in the truck cab until we could feel our fingers and toes again, and then thirteen-year-old Stephen drove us all home in the night.

We didn't get our Christmas tree that day, but we learned a few good lessons about better timing and smarter preparation. Lessons we put to good use down the road as we navigated our way through unconventional life circumstances.

CHAPTER 8

MAKING OUR DREAMS A BIG REALITY

66Are you Canadian?"

The heavyset man with the big grin was obviously enjoying the Grammy nomination party we were hosting at Webster Hall.

"Yes, I am."

"I figured that. Only Canadians could have run a night like this," the man said.

I chuckled and thought to myself, "Maybe he's right, who knows?" I didn't have time to ask him to expound on his insight about Canadians.

But I do know that my Canadian family had enjoyed a long and deep love affair with the glamour and spectacle that was New York City.

Although we were nearly destitute and lived on a farm in the middle of nowhere, my family owned a television set—the only one in our area. This was the 1950s, and we only got one channel. But from time to time, we would see scenes from world-famous New York City on our screen. As kids, we fantasized about the glitz and style of big city life—even if all we knew of the city was from the perspective of Ricky and Lucy Ricardo and their wacky neighbors, Fred and Ethel Mertz.

Our clothes were hand-me-downs, we didn't have shoes, our socks always had holes in them, underwear was scarce, and chores were abundant. All we had was hard work and big dreams. And a feeling that we were destined for greater things.

Steve, my older and rebellious brother, was our inspiration. He made it clear that he wasn't going to be working for strangers or corporations when he grew up. He was going to work for himself and make his own rules. I can still remember the first time he said he was going to be a millionaire, although it didn't mean much to a bunch of kids who plucked pop and beer bottles out of the ditches to earn candy money. We were too busy cleaning pig and cow shit, fetching five-gallon pails of water, and dragging bags of grain to the local mill to be crushed for animal feed to think much about Steve's declaration. Millionaire, yeah, whatever that was.

But Steve's vision and determination inspired us and challenged us and helped lead us off that farm, which we sold in 1974. I was working in real estate by that time and helped arrange the sale, which helped fund the business ventures my siblings and I were already involved in.

We eventually discovered that the nightclub business wasn't so different from what we had been doing all our lives. We worked long hours and cleaned up a lot of shit. Still, getting a chance to create and run some of the hottest nightclubs in the world was a dream come true for these four farm boys—who never lost the ability to eat shit sandwiches while keeping a smile on our faces.

Section Two

IT ALL STARTED WITH PIZZA

> *"You never get caught for doing the crime.*
> *You get caught for doing the crime badly."*
>
> AS HEARD FROM A POLICE OFFICER

CHAPTER 9

PIZZA GAVE US OUR SWAGGER

Although I was never a great student, I did find some success in school. I became the Ontario Public Speaking Champion in high school, and my classmates voted me to be treasurer of the student council. I also served as captain of the high school football and basketball teams. Still, I could not overcome my lack of success in the classroom, and I left school at age nineteen without graduating.

A few years later, I enrolled in a three-week real estate course and secured my real estate license at the age of twenty-one. Within three years, I had worked my way up to be one of the top agents in my area.

As my brothers also finished up their school years, we left the farm one by one but remained close and continued to rely on each other. We had always bonded over business ventures as kids, whether it was collecting bottles or selling apples on the side of the road. And I think our hardscrabble growing-up years had taught us to see potential where others saw only problems.

In fact, our first business grew out of what could have been a very serious problem—getting busted for having a pound of marijuana in

1971. I was twenty-one at the time, living in a small town about thirty miles from our old farm and selling real estate but not really sure what I was going to do with the rest of my life. Fearing we would be facing a hefty fine, we carried several hundred dollars in cash when we went to see the judge about the pot possession. But in a stroke of good fortune that I really can't explain, we got a slap on the wrist!

On our way to celebrate, my brothers and I walked past a restaurant supply store and saw a used Bakers Pride pizza oven for sale. Although I had only recently enjoyed my first slice of pizza, I decided then and there to buy that used pizza oven. I handed the seller $400—the cash I was carrying to pay our expected fine for the weed bust—and promised to return in a month to pay the balance. Now I knew our next move: we would open a pizza parlor!

My impulsive purchase was as crazy as it sounds. We knew nothing about pizza. We knew nothing about running a restaurant. We did not have any property where we could open a pizza parlor. But we had a pizza oven!

In hindsight, it was a bold move and a huge risk, but we had no idea what risks we were taking or how hard it could be. It seems to me that the people who often get things done are the same people who don't know it *can't* be done.

I returned a few weeks later to take possession of our pizza oven. After making the final payment, we loaded it onto our old red truck, although it was clearly too heavy for the vehicle. The police pulled us over after watching us drive by . . . very slowly. But we talked our way out of a ticket and hauled the beast back to the barn on our parents' farm, where it sat until we could find a location for our soon-to-be business.

That spring of 1973 we found an empty storefront in Orangeville, Ontario, that we could rent for fifty bucks on a month-to-month basis. We would locate our pizza parlor at a busy little corner in what had been a beat-up old garage.

Using boards we repurposed from an old barn on the farm and some heat-venting pipes, we needed less than $1,000 to create the cutest little pizza store the town had ever seen. Now we just needed to figure out how to make a pizza.

When I saw a pizza supply truck drive by, I jumped in my battered VW Beetle and chased the truck for ten miles, honking and waving until the driver finally stopped. I told the nice young man behind the wheel that my brothers and I were opening a pizza restaurant and would need supplies. He assured me he could supply us with everything we needed.

Then I told him I had no idea what we needed because we had never made a pizza before and only eaten a few slices of pizza between us in our entire lives. No worries, the driver said. His brother Mario, owned and operated a great pizza restaurant in Brampton, one town over, and he would show us how to make a great pie.

Soon enough, my brothers and I were making our way to Brampton to meet Mario, who taught us how to make the perfect pizza. At the time, we could not afford to buy the mixer we would need to create pizza dough, so we arranged to buy our dough from Mario until we could get our own mixer.

We opened the The Pizza Parlour in October of 1973 using Mario's pizza dough and following his perfect pizza recipe. We made $90 on opening night and thought we were the kings of pizza. Ninety dollars may not sound like a lot, but when you realize that we were charging ninety cents for a full pizza, our opening night receipts were quite impressive!

Pizza was a great opportunity for us, and we made the most of it. We were the Ballinger brothers—young, confident, and ready to take on the world. Pizza is a good business with great mark-ups, and you don't need to be a genius to make it work. What you need to do is make a fabulous pizza, deliver it in a timely fashion, and do it with a smile. The Pizza Parlour was not our first big purchase—that would be the laundromat, which you'll hear more about in an upcoming chapter. But it was our first real business success—if you don't count our apple stand, of course!

By this time, we had all moved into shabby apartments near The Pizza Parlour so we could all pitch in. I would make, sell, or deliver pizza when I could get away from my job selling houses and farms. Steve and Buster—who was only seventeen when we opened—worked there full-time. Gail, who was married to an Orangeville police officer, came in to help even though she had three young kids at home. She organized everything, made delicious pizzas, and added submarine sandwiches to the menu. Peter and my parents helped when they could.

We hired the cutest girls who had the biggest smiles, and we all personally delivered pizza fast and furious until the wee hours of the morning in our fleet of VW Beetles. After starting with a used pizza oven and an unrealistic dream, we soon found ourselves operating the trendiest pizza place in Southern Ontario.

Just two years after we opened The Pizza Parlour, we sold it for $25,000—a lot of money in 1974, especially for a band of dirt-poor brothers who had never run a business. The sale provided us with enough capital to return to our original business venture—the Dundalk laundromat.

It also provided us with an unshakeable sense of confidence and belief in ourselves. After our pizza success, the Ballinger Brothers carried ourselves with a sense of swagger that remains to this day.

CHAPTER 10

DISCO DREAMS AND THE BIRTH OF THE PARTY BOYS

After the sale of the pizza parlor, Steve, Buster, and I decided to splurge on a trip to Mexico. We had never before considered taking a real vacation—let alone one to another country. This trip toward Mexico changed our lives forever.

In February 1976, we rented a small camper and headed south. We were higher than a kite on weed by the time we crossed the border from Canada into the U.S., and we made no attempt to hide our condition. The border officials just looked the other way and let us in. Today, they would arrest us on the spot.

In Tulsa, Oklahoma, we picked up a hitchhiker—again, something that would never happen today. But at the time, it made perfect sense to pick up a fellow traveler. Eventually, our fellow traveler let us in on a secret: he was heading for Mardi Gras in New Orleans while transporting 400 hits of purple microdot acid.

We agreed to take him—and his cargo—to meet his friends in The Big Easy and accepted his generous invitation to tag along and have some fun. Steve, twenty-five, Buster, eighteen, and I, twenty-four, were young enough and crazy enough to think this detour to Mardi Gras was a great idea. (Peter had been smart enough not to join us on this half-baked trip.)

We managed to somehow make Mardi Gras a wilder and crazier place with our very presence, mixing it up in an atmosphere of mayhem, music, overindulgence, kindness, and love. We survived a few brushes with the law and began awakening to what our future might hold for us. After four days of debauchery, we were lucky to leave New Orleans with our lives—and some lessons that would last a lifetime.

We headed through Louisiana and down the coast of Texas until we made it to the Mexican border at Brownsville. The border agents took one look at us and demanded $50 from each of us to let us cross. Something told me this was a bad situation and crossing that border could lead to the kind of trouble we wouldn't be able to get out of. I pleaded with my brothers to turn back and stay in Texas. I told them we could stick around South Padre Island, with its white sand beaches and warm clear waters—and discos.

I think I had them at "discos." We turned away from the border, got cleaned up, and took our little camper to our first big-time disco, something we had only heard about in small-town Canada.

The disco atmosphere captured us immediately under its spell. Beautiful girls, twinkling lights, music, laughter, dancing. But we weren't thinking about just that one night—we were thinking about our future.

The moment we walked in, I told my brothers, "We could do this!"

"The Party Boys" were born that night.

"In the beginning it wasn't the glitz and glamour of the nightclubs, it was the shiny silver coins the laundromat brought in that made it a gold mine."

CHAPTER 11

IT'S A DIRTY BUSINESS

Although the Party Boys came back from Texas with visions of bright lights dancing in their heads, we devoted the next few years to something a lot less glamorous: running a laundromat.

My brother Steve had been sure of his life goals since he was a kid. He was going to be a millionaire, and he wasn't going to spend his life working for someone else. The rest of us boys always idolized Steve, so when he decided to open a laundromat in Dundalk in 1970 we all jumped in with him. Together we could do anything.

Our first step was to rent a space. We chose an old plumber's shop in Dundalk, paying $25 a month on a year-to-year lease from a ninety-year-old widow. We purchased some rickety used laundromat equipment and we fixed up the shop but then ran into a big problem: there was nowhere for the water from the washers to drain. The little town of 750 people had no sewer system.

So we put our laundromat idea on hold temporarily, especially when we stumbled into our pizza opportunity. By 1975, Dundalk's sewer system had been completed, so we were back in business. Using money from our pizza parlor sale, we bought the building that housed the laundromat for $18,000 and renovated the rundown property. The laundromat did not use up all the space, so we converted the rest of the building into a smoke shop and convenience store, where we sold basic groceries and sundries.

The smoke shop idea came from our dad, who said it would work. He was right. The store became a huge hit. Dad and Mom had moved onto a fifty-acre piece of land in a small village about ten miles from Dundalk after we sold the farm in 1974. When we opened our business, Dad worked the counter in the smoke shop and helped us buy stock for the store.

And he taught us a very important lesson about the power of loss leaders: Dad advised us to sell cigarettes for less than we paid for them because he knew we would attract a huge crowd wanting to buy our cheap cigarettes. It seemed like a bad idea to take a loss on every pack of cigarettes we sold, but Dad was right. Because once we got customers in the door with our low-priced cigarettes, they would also buy milk, bread, and other supplies, which all had big markups. Our sales on those items more than made up for what we lost on the cigarettes. Because of Dad's advice, we learned how to harness the power of the loss leader, a lesson we never forgot.

As time went on and the Ballinger brothers continued in business together, we learned which roles each of us was best suited to play, and we played them well. We complemented each other's talents and supported each other's efforts. My role often put me in the spotlight, standing out front and advocating for our businesses, while my brothers were more comfortable in the background, boots-on-the-ground, getting things done. We kept some form of this basic arrangement for the next forty-five years.

We ran our store and laundromat for a couple of years and then sold both in 1977 for $140,000. And this bunch of scruffy young farm boys knew just what we wanted to do with that gold mine.

We were on our way to becoming nightclub impresarios.

Section Three

CHANGING THE NIGHTCLUB CULTURE IN CANADA

"Always leave the other person with their dignity intact, no matter what the circumstances—and especially when doing deals."

CHAPTER 12

BUILDING BALLINGER'S

Even while we were running the store and laundromat in Dundalk, my brothers and I were searching for a big club space to create our own version of a disco. We had not forgotten our experience in Texas, and we were determined to bring some of that party spirit to southern Ontario. We must have visited every run-down hotel and big restaurant in the region before we finally found the perfect place in Cambridge, thanks to a friend. The location was right and so was the price.

During all the years I was helping my brothers run a pizza parlor and laundromat, I was continuing to sell real estate, and I gained a great deal of knowledge about finances and property over those years. We sold the laundromat and convenience store in the spring of 1977 to a young couple for $140,000, a big markup on our initial investment.

We then turned around and bought our dream space out of bankruptcy for $200,000. Our dream property was a two-level site in Cambridge, Ontario, on a slope leading down to the Grand River. The old building had been many things during its storied existence, including a badminton court, dance hall, tavern, and the Highlands Rock and Roll Club. But its best days had been gone for a long time, and the building needed a lot of work. The bank loaned me another $200,000, in part because the manager liked our spunk.

Our goal was to turn the building into Ballinger's Danceteria, the largest dance and video complex in North America. Nothing else like it existed, so we were making it all up as we went. But we never doubted it would work, and we were right. We opened on Halloween in 1979, and Canada's nightlife has never been the same.

We came into Cambridge when we were all in our twenties—fearless, cocky, young, and, some say, very attractive. Word quickly spread through Cambridge that four unknown hot shots had taken over their beloved Highlands Tavern building—and God only knows what they planned to do with it. Pretty young girls came by to check us out and seek jobs, and young guys came to help us out in any way they could. It was like the circus had come to town.

Cambridge was a great and welcoming city of about 60,000 people, and we took it by storm. The young people gravitated to our way of playing music and putting on shows. We came into what others might have called an industrial wasteland and created a big music club full of sword swallowers, cloud swings, high-wire walkers, trapeze acts, go-go dancers, big-name Canadian and American bands, very cool DJs—and our never-ending energy. We made Ballinger's a spectacle—and a huge success.

While running Ballinger's, we started figuring out how to promote our business properly and effectively and which buttons to push, whether we were hyping Halloween, a New Year's Eve party, an out-of-town DJ, or a touring band. We tried everything—from free drinks to free spaghetti and a giant video screen—and most of it worked.

Of course, there was also plenty of drama, some security issues, and—most of all—big problems with some of the rules governing clubs like ours. But in Cambridge, we began to understand that what we were selling was different than the kind of entertainment people would find anywhere else. Recognizing the unique culture of the nightclub business became the key to our success for the next four decades.

"You don't usually find your wife, husband, boyfriend, or lifelong soulmate at a Rolling Stones or Bruce Springsteen concert, but you sure as hell might find them at a nightclub."

CHAPTER 13

WE MADE OUR CUSTOMERS THE STARS

When you go to a Bruce Springsteen concert, a Cirque du Soleil show, a Broadway play, or a movie, you know that you are going to see a performance. You are a spectator enjoying the work of professionals who have spent a large part of their lives building up an amazing set of skills by repeating the same actions over and over until they have honed their craft.

When you go to a nightclub, your expectations about the experience are quite different.

Even if you go to a nightclub to hear a particular act, you as the club customer are going as one of the performers. You wear your cutest outfits and your best shoes. You spruce up your hair and put on the good makeup. You trim your beard to just the right level of stubble and splash on your best cologne. You primp; you preen because you are headed into a music-filled building where *you* are the star. When our family figured out this secret about the nightclub experience, it became easier to make sure that our spaces were always filled with stars!

Nightclubs are also the first responders for hope, fantasy, and maybe even love. Hosting thousands of people every night for decades gave us ringside seats to witness human emotions in their most vivid forms. People from all walks of life and from every place on earth—all who had arrived with their own personal agendas and their own personal burdens—assembled under our roof and surrendered themselves to the magic of music and the crush of the crowds (and the power of whatever substance they were partaking of).

We felt privileged and honored that so many people would go to great lengths to attend our nightclubs. We knew they had worked hard at school or a job all day before they showed up at our place. Maybe they had purchased a new dress or shoes for the occasion. Maybe they had skipped dinner so they would have enough money to get in. Maybe they just wanted to listen to their favorite band on stage that night. Or maybe they wanted to strut their stuff and show off their moves—and yes, their bodies.

Nightclubs were where people went to meet each other. Every night we watched people looking for love. Long before Tinder, Bumble, or Match.com, anyone looking for a one-night stand or a lifelong partner would come to a club like ours.

Two complete strangers could connect for an evening of passion. Assuming they would never see each other again, they would abandon themselves to their desire for wild adventure and physical connection for an evening.

Others came with a similar desire for connection but wanting more than a one-night stand. And many of them found the love of their lives under our lights. Hundreds and hundreds of people have described to me just how they met their husbands or wives at one of our nightclubs. Who knows how many romances we can count as part of our legacy?

To help grease the wheels of romance—and boost the success of our clubs—we hosted a Ladies Night every Thursday for almost forty-two years. We let women in for free and treated them to free drinks and private shows. Most important of all, we protected them from the scoundrels.

We knew there would be no fun and absolutely no party without women in our club. They were our guests, and they were also our business partners because we knew that without the support of women, no nightclub—and maybe no business of any kind—would survive for very long.

So, in the end, one of the Party Boys' most important secrets to success was actually one of the first lessons Mom had ever taught us: treat the women right. And that's what we always tried to do—from The Pizza Parlour to Webster Hall.

"Be nice to everyone on the way up 'cause you're likely to see them again on the way down."

CHAPTER 14

FOOD FIGHT WITH THE GOVERNMENT

Ballinger's was a huge nightclub, sitting all alone between a highway and the magnificent Grand River. We were licensed to include nearly 1,000 people at a time, and it could get crazy busy. We loved handling the party scene, but the food side nearly ate us alive.

According to laws from our conservative provincial government, a place like ours needed to sell almost equal percentages of food and liquor in order qualify for and maintain our liquor license from the powerful Liquor License Board of Ontario (LLBO). We were never really food purveyors—we were Party Boys—and running a first-rate restaurant takes skill and acumen that was far beyond our experience.

We tried to maintain the required food-to-liquor ratio but could not because we were selling dancing, not fine dining. In our first year of business, we made $150,000 from the club part of the business—and lost $150,000 on the food side.

One day in 1980 my brother Steve—for whatever reason—fired the club's only chef for looking at him sideways. (Steve was often full of bluster.) And then Steve left without informing anyone that we no longer had a chef working for us. It was a Friday afternoon a few weeks before Christmas, and I walked into the club to discover we had eighty people with reservations for a Christmas dinner and nothing prepared to feed them.

Acting on pure instincts, I took over the kitchen and conscripted two young bus boys to be my sous chefs. As the orders came pouring, in I tried to stay calm and focused, but the food was a disaster. People complained and some refused to pay for the slop we had served them—and I could not blame them.

That night I decided we would never again be in the food business. We were nightclub operators—not food experts. So I began planning how we could run Ballinger's the way we wanted to while trying to stay within the law. I made some changes to our food and staffing, and we eventually started selling $5 spaghetti buffets—the same price as admission to the club. When customers paid the admission fee, they would get a ticket for the spaghetti buffet, which consisted of a small table filled with rolls, spaghetti, and tomato sauce from a can. We didn't really care if anyone ate the food, we just needed to sell it to get around the LLBO rules. The board was not impressed with our ingenuity.

It also did not like our new operating hours: 8 p.m. till 1 a.m. Wednesday through Saturday. At the time, all licensed establishments were required to be open from 11 a.m. to 1 p.m., seven days a week, which we thought was excessive. Eventually, the local liquor inspector served us a summons to revoke our liquor license.

But we fought back—setting off a battle that would forever change the concept of a Canadian nightclub. I went to talk to a young civil rights lawyer I had read about in the paper. I explained how a young LLBO inspector who didn't much care for me and my brothers had filed to have our license permanently revoked for not selling the proper ratio of food and alcohol and for not staying open as much as the government thought we should. He took our case.

He sued the LLBO, claiming that they did not have the legal right to remove our license and that their rules were unfair. The board had known for years those laws were ludicrous—and it also knew that many business operators were lying on their monthly liquor sales reports. We had just been too young and naïve to know that we *should* lie.

Our young lawyer won our challenge against the LLBO, and soon after, the liquor board rescinded the laws related to opening hours and mandatory food and liquor ratios. A new era of Canadian nightclubs was born.

Ballinger's was no longer burdened by having to sell food or stay open longer hours than necessary. Neither was any other nightclub.

This incident taught me one of the most valuable lessons of my life: when bureaucrats push, push back.

"Always make a point to leave anyplace you inhabit just a little bit better than you found it."

CHAPTER 15

WE MADE SECURITY OUR MAJOR SUCCESS

At Ballinger's, we started acquiring the skills and knowledge we would need to eventually become the best club operators in the world. But there was one lesson we almost didn't live long enough to learn: the importance of security!

Due to our inexperience and need to save money, we initially served as our own security force at Ballinger's. One night, a bunch of Hells Angels and ex-cons beat my brothers and me to a pulp in front of the club. The troublemakers gained entrance into Ballinger's because we had not hired proper security guards who could have stood up to them in the first place.

It was a small town, so everyone knew who had caused the damage. But the pissed-off police veteran who arrived on scene was not interested in arresting the troublemakers. Instead, he turned his fury on me!

In no uncertain terms, the cop told me that I was the mayor of this "town" (the club) and that it was my responsibility to ensure its security. He (accurately) pointed out we had let the perpetrators into our club, taken their money, and sold them booze; but we had no plan for dealing with them when they got stupid with us. He warned me that this could not happen again.

Either you figure out how to run your own club, he said, or the cops would come in and run it for us. "And I guarantee you won't like the way we will run it," he told me.

Point taken.

I immediately hired linemen from the local university's football team and some martial arts experts to be our new security force. We quickly got our security act together, and no one ever again intimidated us at our front doors or inside our nightclubs.

We did call the police again from time to time when it was appropriate, but usually only after we had a bad situation already under control. Over the years we learned that most law enforcement officers are happy to make an arrest when a troublemaker is under control and no longer creating havoc. When the cops recognized that we were running world-class security in our clubs, they were far more likely to respect us and to give us any help we might need.

"Opening and running Ballinger's was like our undergraduate education. We would get our master's and PhD in nightclub management later."

CHAPTER 16

OUR NAME IS ON THE SIGN

My brothers and I poured our hearts and souls into creating Ballinger's. Collectively, we were a great team, and we were tight. We all lived in the old building we had bought, finding little rooms to set up our beds and sharing a communal shower. It was a grand time. We were in our twenties—when anything is possible and your future feels limitless. Together, we believed we could do anything.

We had grown up working together, and we were used to working hard. Even if one of us seemed to be working harder than another brother, we didn't question it. We simply did what had to be done and assumed that one of us would step up to get the job done. We rolled up our sleeves, started a job, and didn't stop until it was finished.

Steve, Buster, Peter, and I complemented each other's skills sets. Steve was fearless and also dynamic, funny, and free spirited. Buster was handsome, charming, and creative. Peter was funny, logical, conservative, and a good businessman. I was fun-loving, a great cheerleader, and knew how to get things done.

We created an immediate buzz in Cambridge when we bought the building that had housed the old Highlands rock 'n' roll club. To help finance the changes we wanted to make, we yanked out a lot of the building's fixtures and offered them up for sale on the side of the road. I painted a piece of plywood with a handwritten "For Sale" message, and then we dragged out old furniture, lights, carpets, bars, glasses, plates and anything else we could get our hands on. I couldn't believe how many people stopped on busy Coronation Boulevard to buy a little something to remind them of the old Highlands club. They probably wanted to check us out, too, since most people in town knew we were planning to open a hip new nightclub soon.

The money we collected from that sale was eye-opening—and not just because we banked $15,000 from stuff we could have sent to the dump. More important, it showed us how passionately interested this energetic little town was in what we were doing.

We had been able to purchase the club for less than expected because the previous owner, a fifty-two-year-old man, had died in the kitchen from being overworked and overstressed. He was just another casualty of the "rough trade" system—which is a label often given to anything related to the music industry.

The previous owner's death did not worry the Ballinger brothers. We were younger and confident we could handle the pressure of being the talk of the town—and, eventually, the whole country. And we did. Those four years we spent in Cambridge, honing our skills for the world stage, were like a master class in everything we needed to take our act to the next level.

We learned and refined our ability to be great promoters and figured out how to employ quirky radio ads and over-the-top posters to draw people into our club. We found out which night club gimmicks—like cigarette girls and stilt walkers—were clever and which were just crazy. Booking great musical acts was definitely *not* crazy, and we perfected the formula for attracting performers like Bryan Adams, Loverboy, Long John Baldry, Ronnie Hawkins, Levon Helm, and the legendary James Brown.

Of course, our best move was to recognize the power of video and the video DJ and take full advantage of this new frontier in the music world. More details about how we hitched our wagon to that shooting star will be revealed in the next chapter.

The big city newspapers, TV, and radio channels were covering us like we were the new nightlife messiahs. We learned quickly to be very careful with the press and not say too much. We wanted to let our shows and work do all the talking and did not want to let a few angry or stupid words haunt us with the public or the press.

We also learned that when you run a business where everyone is either half-dressed or half-drunk it is often better to compromise and roll with the punches. Ballinger's was next to a hospital, near a housing development, and across the street from the river, which we learned carries sound quite well. When our neighbors complained, we turned down the sound system in the middle of our club nights. When the police gave us a "talking to," we shut up and listened. When a young man was beaten up by one of our security guards, we placated his angry older sister, even though the kid had been acting out in a way the guard could not ignore.

The key to success in the entertainment business is to keep a sense of humor, to be empathetic, and to be able to say the right thing or crack a little joke when it's needed most. I always tried to deal with dramas with empathy, humor, and compromise—and sometimes cash. The only time we faced real problems was when we couldn't find our sense of humor in the moment.

Ballinger's in Cambridge was a monstrous success. And it got even bigger when we jumped into the music video scene.

"The nightlife in Canada is where we excelled. Our clubs were all unique, trendy, outrageous, and extremely popular. We were looking for a way to expand that beyond our physical locations."

CHAPTER 17

HOW VIDEO CHANGED EVERYTHING

One of the best moves the Ballinger brothers ever made was to get in on the ground floor of the revolution that brought video to the music industry. Early in our tenure in Cambridge we recognized how video was changing the music scene and started advancing the new art form about the same time as MTV planted its video flag on the broadcast universe.

We first recognized the emergence of a digital culture when our friend "Pin Ball Louie" introduced Ballinger's clubgoers to Pac-Man and Space Invaders around 1980. These original video games were so rudimentary—just horizontal and vertical movements on a flat screen. But lines formed immediately to play these coin-eating whiz kids. The new music video culture was coming hot on the heels of the video game craze, and I soon recognized that we were on the cusp of a burgeoning new digital culture. I suppose a better visionary might have realized we were actually at the very tip of a communication and entertainment revolution that would change the world we Boomers had always known.

I first got a glimpse of what video could do in a nightclub in 1982 at The Ritz—the New York City rock club that years later would become our own Webster Hall. So I contacted Ed Steinberg and RockAmerica, the first company to offer music videos on a subscription basis. RockAmerica created video compilations after securing permission from the musicians and record labels and sold subscriptions to clubs like ours, sending us fresh tapes each month. Initially, we paid $300 a month for one video compilation, but we soon were paying double that price for two reels a month—and those tapes were worth every penny.

In October of 1982 we purchased and installed a huge video screen—the likes of which had never been seen in a Canadian nightclub. It was twenty feet long by fourteen feet wide, and we used it to broadcast our new video collection, including performances by David Bowie, Depeche Mode, Duran Duran, A Flock of Seagulls, Michael Jackson, George Michael, Madonna, Prince, and so many more. The first club in Canada to have such a massive video screen, we positioned it high up in front of our main stage and large dance floor to offer the best view to the most patrons.

This was the start of the video dance music era, the first time in club music history that video performers could replace live music acts—thanks to cutting-edge technology, and Ballinger's was right there on the cutting edge. Kids would show up every night in wild clothes and New Wave hairdos and dance the night away to their favorite music videos. We were proud to be at the forefront of this new phenomenon and to be the first music venue in Canada that was staking out ground in this arena.

Looking back, I now know that the digital music revolution we helped kick off in Canada hastened the end of the old-school, heavy-handed analog music era. The more nimble digital music technology could deliver the new video art and music to the kids in a much cleaner and brighter format.

We did so well at promoting this popular video art form that we had some Canadian TV and radio networks asking to use some of our videos because the American record labels would not share them with Canadian music broadcasters. How did we have these videos? Because I had hidden videos from my newfound RockAmerica source in New York City and spirited them across the border. The American record labels may have been reluctant to share their videos with Canadian broadcasters at that point because they weren't really sure about the legalities. Rules and regulations about who owned music videos and when and how they could be shared were murky back then. Same thing happened years later when people began sharing music files across the internet.

Regardless of the legal intricacies, my brothers and I found ourselves at the forefront of a music movement that was big and getting bigger by the week. We were so sure that we had found something special that in 1982 we changed the name of our Cambridge club from Ballinger's to Ballinger's Danceteria and Videotheque and added the tagline, "The largest dance and video complex in North America."

The experience at Ballinger's Danceteria and Videotheque became the gold standard for a night out in a premium nightclub. Television stations from all over the country came to see our huge nightclub phenomenon. Major Toronto papers sought interviews with us. Our incomes quadrupled.

We then decided to create a weekly dance show, *Canamerica Dance*, to be televised on Canadian stations. We hired an Australian *Penthouse* Pet of the Year and flew her up from New York to host our thirty-minute live show. She was wonderful.

We taped our first show at Ballinger's Danceteria and Videotheque using a format that played five selected videos while beautiful, near-naked go-go girls danced with audience members on our big dance floor. It was such a smash that Toronto's Citytv, the local station run by Moses Znaimer, put *Canamerica Dance* in a prime-time Saturday night slot.

We were flying high by this point. Four little farm boys had single-handedly advanced the biggest musical movement in Canada since the Beatles. And we had even bigger dreams—we wanted TV. And Toronto. And eventually—America.

We decided to sell Ballinger's, by now a near-mythical nightclub, and make our move. After owning Ballinger's for only four years, we were able to sell it in 1983 to a group of Korean businessmen for $1.5 million—more than double our original investment.

Next up: Toronto.

Section Four

THE GOLDEN ERA OF NIGHTCLUBS

"Sometimes bullshit can get you to the top
. . . but it will never keep you there."

CHAPTER 18

THE BEST OF TIMES, THE WORST OF TIMES

In 1984, right after selling our Cambridge, Ontario, super club , we moved to Toronto, ready to bring our unique Ballinger-style entertainment to the big city. We rented warehouse space at 666 King Street West and got to work building our first television studio. Inside the 3,000-square-foot facility we constructed a performance theater, a state-of-the-art editing suite, and first-era analog-to-digital video camera technology.

We had a great idea that we thought would put us at the forefront of the rapidly evolving entertainment world. We eventually learned we didn't have enough experience or deep-enough pockets—or the sense to know we needed more help and better contacts—to make our idea a reality. We had launched our own dance show, *Canamerica Dance*, a first of its kind show featuring videos of pop stars intermingled with club kids dancing while we were still in Cambridge, and we were planning to ride that show into full-time work in the film and television business.

We thought we were on the right track when *Canamerica Dance* was given a plum Saturday night slot on Toronto's Citytv. And we got a boost from the support of Jay Switzer, a forward-thinking Canadian media mogul who believed in our potential. But, sadly, due to our inexperience, I suppose, we never attracted enough sponsors, and we didn't have a bottomless source of income to fully fund the venture.

We knew we couldn't count on our television idea forever, so when our hopes for its success began to dim, we began looking for other ways to earn some money. Then the wealthy man who owned the building that housed our TV studio told us he was dying of cancer. "You guys put so much into your studio," he told us. "You should buy the building 'cause I'm dying and I want a million dollars so I can blow it." How could we say no?

So we purchased the property with the money we had earned on our Ballinger's sale, put our media plans on the back burner, and focused on building a commercial real estate business. In three short years, we bought, retrofitted, and leased out nearly 200,000-square feet of downtown Toronto industrial and retail space. To pull this off, we used up all our club money and began borrowing from the bank.

At the same time, we were creating the most amazing clubs anyone had ever seen. We turned Toronto upside down, leaving a legacy of parties and fun like nothing before or since. We started with The Big Bop and followed that with the Boom Boom Room, Rockit, and The Judicial Museum of Canada. And the young people responded in droves. We were the talk of Toronto night life—if the Ballinger brothers opened a new club, it was going to be hot and it was going to be busy.

But what started with a string of successes crumbled into a plethora of failures in just a few short years. We were hurt by things far beyond our control—like a crippling recession and steep new taxes—but also by our lack of business experience and overall naiveté.

Those years were euphoric and heartbreaking. They also damaged the relationships between my brothers and me, and our general lack of communication became more pronounced. Our struggles in Toronto eventually led us to New York City and three decades of unbelievable success, but I still wish there had been someone around back then to give us better advice and help us avoid some of the worst pitfalls.

The next few chapters will provide more details about our Toronto rollercoaster—what went right and what went wrong. I hope our story can help others avoid our mistakes. And I also hope it can demonstrate that you can recover from such mistakes and emerge even stronger on the other side.

"The people who get real things done are the same people who don't recognize that it can't be done and they just do it. That was always our way. And that's why when you live by the sword you often die by the sword."

CHAPTER 19

THE BIG BOP

When we first got to Toronto, we spent a lot of our energy (and cash) setting up a TV studio and investing in commercial real estate. But we also wanted to bring the same kind of energy and fun we had created at Ballinger's to Toronto. So we went looking for just the right spot for a nightclub.

We found what we were looking for in the former Holiday Tavern—even though the building was run-down and located in one of the highest-crime neighborhoods in Toronto. We gave the space a cool new name—The Big Bop—painted the outside with a rainbow of bright colors, and turned it into a four-story dance club that people talked about for years.

We rented the space for $8,000 a month and spent four months renovating the building's 20,000 square feet. Soon after we opened on June 26, 1986, young people were lining up for two city blocks to get in, even when they had to share the sidewalks with addicts and vagrants.

Toronto had never seen an animal like The Big Bop, which was one of the only Toronto clubs that could hold more than a thousand people. We looked at the old building as our "Oz"—an enchanted kingdom where we could create our own magic.

We boarded up and painted over all the exterior windows and doors and enhanced the mystery by removing all signs. Inside the technicolor building, we created a theme for each floor. From floor to ceiling, each floor had a theme.

On the first two floors, we used fluorescent paints in greens and pinks and painted *The Jetsons* logo on hallway walls. We dedicated those floors to 1960's rock 'n' roll. Legendary DJ Avery, a musical genius, and his sidekick, Joe, were blowing the doors off the giant first floor—it was packed out four out nights a week. On the huge second floor, we hosted the new house music trend, which was becoming the hot new music of its day. The third floor had a running fountain and neon colors accented by black lights, complete with lounge areas where people gathered to commiserate or meditate by our magical neon gardens. Our basement was decorated with technicolor streaks of paint and outfitted with strobe lights to give it an out-of-this-world experience. Young people checking their coats became transfixed with our basement set-up.

Maybe that is why our basement coat check became so popular. In our first month of operations, we had so many patrons using this simple service that it made enough money to cover the entire rent for the whole month. Those numbers proved to us that we had Toronto's young people eating out of our hands.

Instead of apologizing for the Big Bop's seedy location, we made it a part of the club's mystique. We ran edgy ads on the local hip CFNY radio station. With the sound of wind and lightning in the background, a low, deep voice would invite listeners to "Take a walk on the wild side and step over a derelict into a four-story funhouse located at the hard end of the Queen West Village in the part of Toronto that never sleeps."

We knew that young people are always striving to find something new and unique and maybe even a bit scary. If you can pique their interest and curiosity with something innovative, they will come, even if—or maybe because—you are on the wrong side of the tracks. After our five years in Cambridge, we were seasoned, mature club owners, yet we still possessed the youthful exuberance needed to turn this inner-city blight into the hottest entertainment venue in Toronto.

People asked, who are these guys? How was this group of unusual, but cool-in-their-own-way, clever, swashbuckling brothers from the sticks managing to draw thousands of people to a neighborhood that had only known heartache and desperation for many, many decades? Our success blazed a trail for dozens of others to pursue, and it wasn't long until this area became synonymous with cool and cutting-edge restaurants, cafes, clubs, and fashion-culture denizens—all thanks to the Party Boys.

By 1987 The Big Bop was open four nights a week (Wednesdays through Saturdays) and we were making more than $60,000 in cold cash per week with a $5,000 payroll and an $8,000 monthly rent. With the money rolling in, we bought more real estate and built more nightclubs.

And the game was on.

"Threes get threes and eights get eights, and that's the way it's always been. Unless there is money involved."

CHAPTER 20

TEACHING TORONTO HOW TO CREATE NIGHTCLUBS RIGHT

Building on the success of The Big Bop, we created a brand and a way of doing things that was soon recognized as visionary across Toronto. We chose architecturally interesting buildings in run-down neighborhoods and transformed them both. Our clubs featured multiple floors and multiple styles of music all under one roof—like the parties we attended as teens in big, old farmhouses.

Using the formula that made The Big Bop a hit, we opened four other clubs in the city between 1985 and 1990—the Boom Boom Room, The Rocket, The World, and the breathtaking, 20,000-square-foot Go-Go nightclub with the city's first rooftop patio that eventually launched Toronto's new entertainment district. Unfortunately, we didn't get to finish the Judicial Museum of Canada before the recession wiped us out.

Of course, our clubs showcased great DJs, good sound, and state-of-the-art visual effects. We had learned the art of front-door etiquette, and we also created a unique vibe as we liked to pack people in *snugly*. We arranged our interior layout so that patrons would have to squeeze by one another to get around—it was part of the plan. We obviously encouraged audience participation and interaction (and dancing and drinking) because we wanted everyone to have a good time. We never consulted with designers or fashionistas; we simply chose our own décor and painted the walls so that everyone would feel comfortable and not worry about making a mess.

We also hosted unique nightly theme parties—Wednesday was Depression night with low-cost drinks, and Thursday was Ladies Night with free admission and drinks for women. Those exceptionally curated theme night always attracted big crowds especially women, who where always our superstars. Maybe most important, we provided a place where you could be yourself, feel safe yet be free, and let your hair down and meet people from all walks of life on equal footing.

The young people validated our vision by flocking to our venues.

We also created or reimagined other spaces, including the cutting-edge Royal Kinghurst Fashion Centre and the unique Hotel Heartbreak. Our coup de grâce was going to be the eye-popping Judicial Museum of Canada, a property we built from Toronto's very first courthouse at 57 Adelaide Street. We had completed about 90 percent of our planned renovations to the 1850 building before our financial crash put a stop to everything.

Our plan was to create a museum that would double as an entertainment facility, providing spaces for people to dance and places where they could learn more about Canadian legal history and crimes. We were including basement jail cells that would tell the story of Canadian lawbreakers who had influenced our legal system and help us understand how we became Canadians with our own unique history and system of justice.

For example, the last woman hung behind this building was punished because she had defended herself from her husband's beatings. In the 1880s, Canadian law allowed men to beat their wives as long as their rods were no bigger then a broomstick. The planned museum/nightclub combination was a masterpiece that no one but us understood, and it is a shame for Toronto that we never got to finish it before our heartbreaking collapse forced us to move. Sadly, we often heard from Canadian friends that nothing cool in nightlife ever happened in Toronto again after the Ballingers left for New York City.

To continue to buy and renovate properties, we leveraged our assets but made the mistake of getting our financing from a huge American bank that pulled out of Canada at the height of the recession in 1990. The move left us high and dry and with nowhere to turn, so we folded up our clubs and left for New York.

Fortunately, we didn't lose the Ballinger brothers' best asset—which was the unique set of talents we each brought to the party. Buster was the set designer, Steve managed construction, and I handled finance and marketing. Peter was funny, logical, conservative and probably the best businessman of us all. We had an unspoken philosophy that if you passionately believed in a project, you should get it started and the rest of us would essentially (yet often silently) back your efforts. Although we often clashed, even those disagreements pushed us to do our best work and work hard.

Our formula worked well—until it didn't.

"We learned that combining a lack of experience with taking on more than you can chew—as well as assuming others will be as patient as you are—can end badly."

CHAPTER 21

THE CLIMB WAS GREAT; THE FALL WAS SPECTACULAR

We opened the Big Bop in the middle of 1986 and were soon pulling down tens of thousand of dollars per week—more than we had ever dreamed possible. In the next few years, we opened four more nightclubs and invested in more real estate than I can recount. Just a few years after arriving in Toronto, we had become superstar club owners and hot-shot real estate developers with a golden future.

We were so confident that our fortunes would continue to rise that we did not notice the dark clouds forming on the financial horizon or consider how they might affect us. It never occurred to us that our full-speed-ahead mentality could be dangerous. But it turned out that never taking our foot off the gas when building our "empire" put us in a tough spot when things went south.

The American economy collapsed in 1987 and took Canada with it, and we were caught flat-footed. We were floating about $5 million in renovation loans for our real estate holdings at that time, a lot of money, and we watched in trepidation as our annual interest rate rose to over twenty-one percent.

Around the same time, Canada began imposing a new nine percent tax on goods and services. The increase in taxes and interest rates had a massive impact upon Canadian's disposable and actual incomes. Suddenly, tenants in some of our beautifully renovated commercial properties stopped paying rent, which meant we could not pay our mortgages or the city's high real estate taxes, and everything we knew began to unravel.

In less than a year, we went from "kings of the castle" to "bums in the basement." We lost everything we had created in Toronto, but I learned a valuable lesson: You really can't trust anybody and nobody but you even cares. I never forgot that lesson moving forward.

Nevertheless, I did everything humanly possible to try to redeem myself and my family. I worked incredibly hard to straighten things out with our banks and debt holders. But eventually, my lawyer of many years told me, "Let go, Lon. It's over. It's time to leave."

So I went to the banks, the borrowers, the tenants, and the staff, and reconciled with them. Even though this failure haunts me to this day, I am proud that we were never sued for a nickel because of our honesty and our straightforward negotiations.

With our Canadian business empire in tatters, we turned our eyes south. In 1988, during our real estate buying spree, we had purchased the old Webster Hall building (or, at least we thought we purchased it—more details on that situation in a later chapter) and poured a lot of money into renovating the property. We now centered our hopes on making a new start in New York City. But things weren't looking good there, either, because we had not been able to secure a liquor license.

It was a sad time for us all. My self-esteem was tied to my business success, so my fall from the top of the world led me to the bottom of a bottle.

The pressure took me to the breaking point. I couldn't sleep and my beautiful head of hair fell out in huge chunks. I drank heavily and disappointed my family and myself. My resolve withered away, month by month, and I couldn't even complain because I knew I had helped create this mess: I had not built my foundations strong enough to withstand a financial storm. And I also knew I had to find a way to keep going for my wife and our three little kids. Lois and I had been together since 1971 and married since 1983, and I was determined to find a good way to support my family.

I knew then we would soon be leaving for America, and we would never return. And we haven't, except to occasionally visit friends and family. When asked if I'll ever go back to Canada, I always joke and say, "No, the trees are too short, and the land is too flat." But in reality, we left a big part of our hearts behind in that great country, and we are grateful for all the lessons we learned there. Many of the people we left helped provide the knowledge and wisdom and courage we needed to make a fresh start in the Big Apple.

Looking back on this time of my life, I wish someone had been able to give me the advice I now offer here. Here are the most important lessons I learned from this difficult period of my life.

- Be careful in your search for wealth. Being comfortable and having financial peace of mind is a worthy life goal, but if you put too much effort into seeking great worth, you will lose valuable time with your family.
- Do not tie your self-worth to your net worth.
- Don't forget all your childhood dreams in a single-minded quest for success.
- Good friends often disappear when they think all you care about is wealth and prestige.
- Striving to be financially comfortable—rather than excessively wealthy—will leave you with time for your family, your interests, your friends, and new ideas and adventures to explore.

After my frantic efforts to stop the financial collapse of our Canadian holdings and my months of failure-related despair, I quit drinking. I realized my drinking had contributed to some of our problems because I had not always been at the top of my game or as focused as I should have been.

When I got sober, I felt like I had been rescued from the clutches of greed and avarice. Instead of becoming some rich, nasty, greedy man who thought he owned the world on the last trip, I could now focus on becoming a better leader, a better father, and—frankly—a better person.

"Leaving Toronto for New York City was a big adventure and sure took the edge off of the Toronto collapse—and at the time it's exactly what was needed."

CHAPTER 22

HEADING FOR THE WORLD'S BIGGEST STAGE

When we realized there was no way we even wanted to rescue our Canadian empire, we turned our sights to New York City and Webster Hall, although we knew that leaving Toronto behind and heading to New York City would not solve all our problems. In fact, we were trading one set of challenges for another.

Our liquor license application for Webster Hall had been denied twice, so we weren't even sure we would have a business to run in New York. In addition, the property owners had reneged on the sale of the building to us and now were refusing to grant us a long-term lease. Instead, the landlord would only grant a month-to-month agreement. Can you imagine how nerve-racking that was?

In New York, I spent my days managing the homeless people, prostitutes, and drug dealers who lived in front of Webster Hall. We all worked hard to make sure we would be ready to open a new club if we ever got our liquor license and other problems ironed out. Let's face it, if I failed I would not be in much better shape than the people living on the street around me. Were we crazy?

Maybe. But we were again looking at our work as a big and exciting adventure. We had lost our shirts in Toronto in part because we already had our eyes on Webster Hall. In retrospect, I am certain we could have stayed and rescued at least some of our Toronto nightclubs and properties. But we chose to head to the Big Apple instead because at this time we were young, fearless, and hell-bent on being the best nightclub operators in the world. And we felt that you could never claim that title unless you were in New York City.

We had dreamed about New York City from the time we were little kids watching TV specials, and now we were ready to see if we could make it work there. Everyone but Peter, that is. He decided Canada was where he belonged, so he stayed behind. While Peter was quietly creating a path to becoming a gentleman farmer and a multimillionaire investor, Steve, Buster, and I were forging our way through the bright lights and dark alleys of New York City nightlife.

Our many successes—and failures—in four short years in Toronto had given us way more confidence about running Webster Hall if we got the chance. We had perfected club security and regular club crowd control and we had learned how to develop working relationships with the police and fire department.

We had mastered marketing and knew our theme nights and publicity campaigns would work wherever we went. We had discovered what type of building, neighborhood, and staff were ideal for the type of club we wanted to run. And we learned not to take on too much too fast—which may have been the most important lesson of all.

We knew some people would wonder if these Canadian dudes had just fallen off the turnip truck in New York City. But we were confident we could quickly prove our doubters wrong. We were world-class warriors who had been through every battle imaginable in our line of work, and we were more than ready for whatever Gotham could throw at us.

Or so we thought.

Section Five

CONQUERING NEW YORK

"What we recognized about that tired, worn-out, old building was its history. Upon further inspection, we learned at one time it had been an RCA recording studio that led to the birth of stereophonic music. The Henry Mancini Orchestra were the first recording artists to create a stereophonic record. That's when we knew that Webster Hall was not going to be our club; it was going to be New York City's club."

CHAPTER 23

HOW TO BUILD A NEW YORK CITY SUPER CLUB

While we were building our nightclub business in Canada, we were also looking for the perfect New York City location where we could share our talents. When I first heard the old Ritz building in the East Village of Manhattan was for sale, I hopped on the next plane from Toronto to New York City to meet the real estate agents.

The old building really was painted shades of gray and pink, and the pigeons really were flying through it. But it was love at first sight. Built in 1886 as a "hall for hire," the four-story structure had been hosting social events of all kinds for more than a century. Booze, beer, dancing, and music had been the cornerstone of this building long before we were born.

A little research revealed that the building had seen all kinds of political rallies, weddings, meetings, fund-raisers—and, of course, concerts and dances—in its lifetime. In the 1950s, RCA had established Webster Hall Studios as its East Coast recording venue, and everyone from Elvis to Julie Andrews had recorded there. Bob Dylan made his recording debut by playing harmonica on a Harry Belafonte album in that building.

Its most recent incarnation had been a rock club called The Ritz, which had been one of my favorites nightclubs whenever I visited New York City in the early '80s. It was run by Jerry Brandt and Marty Diamond, who were brilliant bookers and operators. Jerry Brandt had brought video to The Ritz in the early 1980s, and his club had helped inspire us to bring music video to Ballinger's in Cambridge.

But The Ritz had not utilized all four floors of the building, and my brothers and I wanted all four floors—with about 10,000 square feet on each floor. The building badly needed to be renovated, and we saw a clean slate that we could transform into our type of club.

The owners of the building were members of a cultural organization representing people from Galicia, Spain, and they were immediately attracted to our Canadian politeness and charm. The owners selected our bid over thirty-nine other offers—in part because we offered them a loan they never paid back of $250,000 to help them fight a lawsuit with the previous tenants. That moved us to the front of the line to purchase the Webster Hall building once the suit had been settled.

But these same landlords eventually reneged on their promise to sell the building to us, offering us only a month-to-month lease. But by the time we understood the depths of the deception, Webster Hall had become our most significant hope for rebuilding our reputation and our nightclub business.

We learned that nothing we had done up to this moment could have really prepared us for New York City. We were somewhat naïve and truly ignorant of the unwritten rules that governed New York City at that time—and still do today, to some extent. Our Canadian experiences and good names meant nothing here. It was an uphill battle, and the lawyers we hired did not provide a lot of help with the somewhat devious landlords—or with our more formidable foe: the community board.

"When it comes to community relations, always take the high road. Work to find compromises. Do all you can to win over your critics over with kindness and respect. "

CHAPTER 24

KILLING THEM WITH KINDNESS

Anarchy reigned in the East Village in the 1980s. Drugs, theft, murder, prostitution, homelessness, and decay were in full display on every street, and laws were rarely enforced. Many stores were empty, and burned-out buildings were omnipresent in the neighborhood around Webster Hall. We knew a thriving nightclub like the one we planned to run could help improve the neighborhood because we had seen that happen in Toronto.

But we had to convince the neighbors of the benefits of our vision. Specifically, we had to convince the local community board because we could not apply for a liquor license unless we had their approval. And the community board was *not* inclined to give their approval to a bunch of Canadian "Party Boys."

It didn't help that The Ritz—the club we wanted to replace—had a reputation as a notoriously bad neighbor. It apparently had racked up hundreds of violations from the police, fire department, state liquor authority, and building inspectors. There were even reports of at least four deaths caused by misadventure and negligence.

We spent nearly two and a half years attending monthly meetings of the community board, hoping to win their trust, but were shocked and dismayed by the name-calling and veiled threats that were routinely thrown our way by what we now recognize as organized malcontents driven by political agendas. Coming from Canada, we had never witnessed such vitriol or organized viciousness.

We didn't realize back then that there was a lot more going on behind the scenes than what we were seeing at those meetings. The community board is designed to give residents a voice in their neighborhood for current activities and future developments, but—in my opinion—this board was really answering to shrewd political figures. Sheldon Silver, a powerful New York politician who died in prison after being convicted of corruption charges, was very influential in the East Village during this era. In Russia, nothing moves unless Putin approves of it. In the East Village, nothing moved unless Sheldon approved of it, and I suspect he was involved in our bitter battles with the community board.

Conniving, unscrupulous people continuously challenged our existence, and Webster Hall was almost suffocated before it ever was ever born. The community board cloaked themselves as saviors of the neighborhoods, but meetings were the home to subtle kickbacks and payoffs for mysterious players who lurked in the corners of the local community. I realize my assessment is tough, but it's truthful. We came hat in hands to their meetings and left battered and bruised every time. Decades later, I'm still bitter at how we were treated.

What we didn't know at the time was that board members were also being solicited by other individuals and groups who were seeking the old building for their own purposes. Webster Hall was in the G6 zoning area, which allowed for uses like nightclubs and gambling centers, but the neighborhood had also been opened to some residential units because of a massive housing shortage. The mixed use made it extremely difficult to settle questions of how much noise was allowable and how many clubgoers would be acceptable. Music venues had been dodging zoning bullets for years, and the community board always came with challenges from sources you never knew even existed.

We tried to reassure the board and our would-be neighbors of our intentions. We explained that we wouldn't abandon the property because owning and operating this business was the only way we had to feed our families. We promised we would be a good addition to the neighborhood—if we were only given the chance. We wanted to brighten it up, not bring it down.

Finally, in June 1992 after two years and several rejections, the community voted 16-to-14 vote to allow us to apply for a liquor license. And in July of 1992, the state liquor authority granted us a liquor license, allowing us to open in October of that year.

To Canadian businessmen, New York City real estate and zoning was a different world with many layers of unknown. Multiple parties had their own agendas, and all the parties had lawyers who could stop normal wheels of progress by mounting legal challenges to tie up movement of any type. It took us three years and a Canadian financial bloodbath to get all the necessary licenses and approvals to open Webster Hall. But in the end, perseverance and dreams won out.

And in the coming years, we discovered that our most important community relationship meetings were held by the local police precinct. Precinct 9 was famous for handling a diverse and mostly poor group of residents, and the precinct's monthly affairs meetings included all members of the area. We were sure to never miss one of those meetings because we knew they weren't tainted by political agendas. Not many people attended these meetings, but we knew the people who showed up were actual community members and that it was important for our survival to be there every time.

We seldom spoke and we never complained. But if a community member took issue with anything regarding Webster Hall, the police would tell us to meet with the complainant and deal with their problem. Through this process, we learned that what most complainers really wanted was to know someone was listening to them.

As decades went by, the complaints disappeared, and we became a trusted and valued member of the new East Village culture. The drug dealers and vagrants left and were replaced by hip little businesses and a vibrant new population. And Webster Hall was at the center of it all.

"We loved booze, fun, sex, music, and all the things young men fantasize about. What made us different was our ability to turn our fantasies into a reality, and opening night at Webster Hall was the culmination of a dream come true."

CHAPTER 25

THE START OF THE GREATEST PARTY ON EARTH

After three years of hanging on by the skin of our teeth while fighting for our rights in the bureaucratic maze of New York City regulatory boards and community councils, the Party Boys from Toronto flung open the doors to Webster Hall on October 2, 1992.

We knew we were bringing our unique vision of a nightclub to a world hungry for something new and were excited that the public would finally get a glimpse of the space we had been preparing for them. The weather that evening was picture perfect, and family and friends were all there to share this magic moment, including my mother, who would become a nightly fixture in front of the club.

Suzanne Bartsch, the Swiss diva who was in icon of New York nightlife, had helped make this opening night party a stunning spectacle. Using her magical skills and plumbing her best guest lists, she helped us gather the most incredible group of citizens and entertainers who would produce an eye-bulging cornucopia of lust, pleasure, music, dancing, laughter, love, and hope.

Shortly after we opened our doors, our four-story musical funhouse was packed with almost 5,000 people. White, black, Latino, big, small, fat, rich, poor, straight, gay, famous, unknown—and all outrageous. People were having sex on the big stage in the grand ballroom. Anthony Kiedis of the Red Hot Chili Peppers was dancing round houses on the floor. High-wire walkers, sword swallowers, stilt walkers, and magicians were tossing and turning high above the crowds. Beautiful women were strutting throughout the massive structure wearing nothing but high heels and little black cat masks. Muscle man and the Chelsea boys were bumping and grinding their massive physical bodies.

Anyone lucky enough to get into Webster Hall that night was experiencing the most hedonistic night in the history of the one of the most hedonistic cities on earth.

But I wasn't inside at the party. I was out front trying to make sure the Greatest Party on Earth didn't end before it had a chance to get started. Because even after we had packed thousands of people into our four stories, 10,000 more were milling around outside, annoying the cops and infuriating our neighbors. The red brick walls of Webster Hall seemed ready to burst; the winding stairways were so packed that you could hardly move from one massive floor to another. Outside, streets were gridlocked as would-be partygoers tried to get to Webster Hall.

"George Wayne will not be left outside for one second more," screeched Suzanne, who had done so much to make our opening night a success. She was trying to make sure the well-known celebrity columnist could get inside. "I will not have my reputation smeared."

My brothers and I were standing at the front door, mouths agape, somewhere between shocked, overwhelmed, and concerned. The police had just informed us that if we let one more person into this madhouse they would close us up for good before we even had a chance to start. But what would happen if we turned away thousands of New York City's most colorful night-lifers?

That night we learned how clever and fair the New York Police Department could be. They knew our backs were against the wall, and they worked with us to make sure we could admit as many people as possible and turn away others without starting a riot.

The police were willing to work with us because they knew how hard we had been working over the past three years to transform this old building and this gloomy, crime-riddled street. They had watched us clean garbage and filth from the sidewalks to show our respect for the neighborhood. They knew we had given money to help relocate some of the homeless people who had been sleeping on the street. They had seen us transform a decrepit old building where pigeons roosted into a glittering house of fun that thousands of people wanted to explore.

Fortunately, the police recognized that under our wild boy exteriors beat the hearts of true professionals. The cops also knew how important night life was to NYC and recognized how a popular nightspot could help transform a whole neighborhood.

The area around Webster Hall had been reeling for decades from bankruptcies, homelessness, desperation, filth, and neglect. So had New York City. October 2, 1992, marked a renaissance that the building, the neighborhood, and the city had been waiting for. For the next twenty-five years, Webster Hall became a beacon of light for a city that was also growing safer, more confident, and more diverse. From that night on, people would say, "As Webster Hall goes, so goes New York City." That is to say, you could gauge the vigor of the City by looking at Webster Hall to see if we were busy or soft. We had created that kind of hold on the naked city.

When I look back at opening night and think about the thousands who were inside and the thousands more who were outside, I'm still not sure how we worked everything out without causing a riot outside or experiencing serious damage. But like every other improbable step in this venture, it all worked out okay. Somehow. What I know for sure is that Webster Hall's opening night was a colossal success, and it set us on the road for an incredible run.

For the next twenty-five years, my family brought millions of people together on what was once the most crime-riddled street in the East Village. We created a dream world of fantasy, history, music, and lights ensconced in a labyrinth of worn stairways, and mysterious spaces where people of all walks of life could enjoy four floors of wonderfully diverse people and dance music entertainment.

We helped thousands of people enjoy themselves for a night and/or find a lifelong mate while also helping advance the careers of so many young musicians, including Lady Gaga, Halsey, Adele, Cage the Elephant, Guns N' Roses, Travis Scott, Skrillex, and so many more. We were the official nightlife destination for all New Yorkers and for thousands of tourists visiting the city. We hosted the giant East Village Halloween afterparty for years and also supported the highly respected annual Global music festival.

We never wanted Webster Hall to be a club just for rich white people who were too boring and too entitled. Instead, we wanted it to be as culturally, socially, and financially diverse as New York City itself. From day one, we set out to make Webster Hall into a New York City icon, just like the Statue of Liberty or the Empire State Building.

That crazy opening night helped set us on the path to reach those crazy goals.

"Women don't need men. Men need women. Nightclubs would not even exist without women power."

CHAPTER 26

EVERY NIGHT SHOULD BE LADIES NIGHT

From our first night at Ballinger's we knew no nightclub could survive without the affection and support of women. Our mother had always taught us to put ladies first, and we obeyed her rule at Ballinger's, in our Toronto clubs, and especially at Webster Hall.

After decades in the nightclub business, I am convinced that women are the social bosses. Just clear out of the way, boys, and let the ladies run the show. Women can have fun by themselves—men, not so much. Attract the women to your business, and the men will follow. Focus on making your female customers happy, and everything else in your business (and life) will fall in line.

Of course, every Thursday night was Ladies Night at our clubs, where women got in for free and received free drinks. Sometimes we held private shows for their eyes only, and we gave them roses as they left the club, which made them feel a little loved and totally respected.

But the most important way we showed women that they were our priority was to make them feel safe. We did our best to keep out the scoundrels who had no good intentions. But knowing we could never catch them all, a helpless woman was never left alone at Webster Hall.

I'm not sure I ever saw a totally helpless woman at our clubs. Even if they had inadvertently overindulged, we discovered most women were resourceful enough to maintain a network of support. But a building constructed in 1880 had a lot of hiding places where someone might unwittingly wind up in a bad spot, so we had forty security guards—both men and women—patrolling the club relentlessly, looking for troublemakers and keeping an eye out for vulnerable women.

If they found a woman who had overindulged or fallen asleep, they would not let a man near her unless he could prove he was a partner or a close friend. Our strict, tough-as-nails security team would guard the woman until her friends could be found or we had enough information to secure her a taxi ride home.

Our protect-the-women policies and proactive security unit won the respect of the police—and more importantly, the women.

Truth was, every night at Webster Hall was ladies night, and making women a priority helped make it the greatest party on earth and helped make us New York's go-to spot.

"Often you realize that the best thing you ever did was the thing that you didn't do."

CHAPTER 27

RUN YOUR BUSINESS PROFESSIONALLY

When we arrived in New York City, we weren't really the country bumpkins we often portrayed ourselves to be for the media. We weren't bad boys either—but we *were* party boys. And we never expected that everyone we attracted to our club would be squeaky clean. We were in the nightclub business after all.

However, there were limits to what we allowed to go on, and sometimes we had to step in and say enough is enough—especially when it came to the drug scene. Drugs have always played a huge role in music and particularly in nightlife, but they have also led to the downfall of many artists—and the businesses that surround those artists. So the Ballinger brothers made a choice early on to remain friendly to those who dabbled but not embrace the drug culture.

We chose to draw our boundaries partly because nightclubs were the way we made a great living, and the success of our nightclubs relied on the sale of alcohol. We never wanted to do anything that would threaten our ability to legally sell alcohol, and we were clever enough to not be sneaky and greedy like most of the other nightclub guys of that era.

But our refusal to fully welcome drugs and drug dealers and drug culture into Webster Hall was also about our desire to create a great club for "the average person." Other famous New York clubs catered to the rich and entitled who could afford cocaine and ecstasy or the other popular drugs of the day, but we chose not to rely on drugs, dealers, or the people they attracted.

Instead, we chose a route that allowed us to provide a far more interesting—and safer—experience than other big clubs of the era. The average person who came to Webster Hall could enjoy a safe and great nightlife experience with our four floors of different New York-centric dance music, spectacular high-wire walkers, trapeze acts, tarot card readings, stilt walkers, snake charmers, breathtaking lights, sweet smooth sounds, and—of course—the beautiful staff. As a result, we always had lines two city blocks long at our "average person" nightclub with our "free-before-midnight" admission policies.

We outhustled every other club that set up shop and buried them all with our great circus shows, go-go dancers, and unusual layout. And we did it all legally. We stayed at the top so long because we paid our taxes, listened to the cops, and respected our neighbors while never forgetting to serve a great product to our customers. We realized our survival in this business depended on following the laws and codes of the police and the fire department and the building inspectors and the neighborhood groups and the state liquor authority. Yes, we were put in the penalty box from time to time, but we were never suspended from the league.

As Baby Boomers ourselves, my brothers and I witnessed the evolution of the drug culture in North America. We grew up when alcohol and cigarettes dominated the social scenes of the 1950s and then and watched as the cycle of amphetamines and downers became part of the work and leisure culture of the 1960s. We were teenagers when marijuana and heroin became heavy hitters by the mid 1960s. By the time we were running nightclubs in the late 1970s, cocaine and MDMA—later known as ecstasy—saturated that world.

Of course, we knew various performers we booked would attract different types of crowds who favored different types of substances. But we tried not to encourage anything or anyone that would upset the rhythm we created for the average clubgoer. The average person always came first in our world.

Even so, sometimes our efforts veered off track.

One night in the late 2000s, we hosted a huge party called the Day Glo. We knew this was going to be the ultimate "experience," so worked diligently to prepare our staff and security. Although we thought had prepared adequately, we were overwhelmed when the crowds began arriving by the busload.

Soon, there were over 8,000 kids all dressed in white—stoned out of their minds on ecstasy—trying to get into Webster Hall. It was bizarre. These kids were planning to enter the club, get soaked in neon paint, and dance their butts off while hugging and laughing like hyenas on uppers.

We quickly lost control and called the police for help. To their credit, the police came into the crowd on horseback and gently but firmly told the massive crowd of joyous kids that the event was oversold and they wouldn't be getting into the club that night. Instead of screaming and yelling, all those kids really wanted to do was hug the police and pet their horses. They were having just as much fun on the street as they could have had in the club.

The cops recognized quickly this mob of characters dressed in white and hugging little teddy bears weren't in the least bit violent or belligerent. They were just so obviously high on MDMA that all they wanted to do was hug somebody. The crowd was dispersed, and life went on.

We faced a similar storm a few years later, in 2016, when outdoor performances at the Governor's Ball on Manhattan's Governor's Island—including one by Kanye West—were canceled due to inclement weather. When West and Kim Kardashian decided to drop into hip-hop's favorite big-league club, tens of thousands of young people decided to join them, descending upon Webster Hall on a hot Sunday evening in droves. You can read more about that incident in our chapter on VIPs, but let's just say that on that night, we once again were incredibly grateful for the NYPD!

As we learned and relearned over our decades in the nightclub business, the one part we couldn't really control was how many people would be drawn to our clubs on a given night. We also couldn't control what drugs they might have taken before arriving. That was one reason we took our security very seriously.

We also couldn't control which people would want to visit our clubs on a given night—as I explain in the next chapter. That was another reason we took security very seriously.

"Always walk lightly, talk softly, and
carry a big stick—just in case."

CHAPTER 28

THE MANY "GANGS" OF NEW YORK

66 You could be the president of the United States, Lon," Manhattan District Attorney Robert Morgenthau told me once as we lunched in his private suite in his favorite Italian restaurant. "You have to get along with both the good guys and the bad guys and you seemed to have figured that part out," he said.

I never thought too much of that comment until I started writing this book. I realize now he was probably onto something. At Webster Hall, we hosted huge events and fundraisers for politicians and musicians and entertainers of all stripes. We also dealt with major issues from all the bad-guy groups. We learned the art of survival by knowing when to duck and how to compromise. How to leave everyone with a little something so they all could go home in peace. Compromise and resolution for everyone and everything must be at the top or near the top of every good business's strategy.

Over the years, we had interactions with almost every collection of misfits and malcontents New York ever gave roots to. From our landlords to loyalists from other nightclubs to the mob and the Hells Angels and Albanian death squads, the one thing they all had in common was misplaced anger and strength in numbers.

When we arrived in the East Village in 1992, downtown was under siege from crack addicts and homeless encampments and other lawless kooks, and goofy Mayor Ed Koch seemed powerless to do anything about it. All types of troubled folks roamed 11th Street at the time. We quickly learned about the power of the "gang." What I'm calling "gangs" are groups of humans who knew how to behave badly for profits as long as they have lots of loyal, likeminded lowbrows to back them up.

Gangs we encountered included community boards, the mafia, and packs of young men who controlled certain territory. To survive the myriad gangs who came at us in New York, we had to learn how to divide and conquer and to be ready to fight fire with fire if necessary.

Our preferred move was always to find the ringleader of a group and quickly seek to forge a peaceful solution to their perceived gripes. When we identified the ring leaders, we could apply the street smarts we had learned so well in Canada—beginning with our days battling bullies in our hometown. We knew how to stick up for ourselves and each other, and we avoided calling the cops unless it was absolutely necessary.

Our first move was to determine whether a gang was with us or against us—and that often boiled down to whether we paid them or not. But we had to choose our position wisely, regardless of whether the organization we were facing was lawful or lawless.

All of the gangs we tangled with taught us lessons, and we taught them a few things, too. Here are the stories from some of the gangs we faced.

THE MOB

The first nefarious group we ever tangled with—other than our long-time landlords—turned out to be part of the New York mob. They were working as tradesmen on a big movie theater that was being built from a nearby burned-out garage while we were getting Webster Hall ready to open. One day, a group of the tradesmen stopped my brother Buster and asked him who was doing the work on our building.

My beautiful and clever little brother told them we were doing the work. The men quickly surrounded him and began shouting and shoving him back and forth between them like they were playing a game of human pinball. This was 1989, so Buster was young and agile enough to escape and get himself back into the empty nightclub to tell us what had just happened. Needless to say, it caused us to become a bit uneasy.

Fortunately, we had hired a small contractor from Queens named Rudy. We called Rudy the master of the $700 job because he booked hundreds of small repair jobs all over Manhattan. Rudy, who had taken a liking to us, told us not to worry. "I'm going to talk to somebody about this and we will see what we can do."

As it turned out, Rudy apparently had some influence with someone in the mob hierarchy. (Rudy told us he had killed a man for them long ago, but we weren't really sure we believed that story.) Rudy convinced the mob that we weren't doing any construction that would require plumbers or electricians, and because of their respect for Rudy, I guess, they left us alone from that point on.

THE GALICIAN LANDLORDS

Webster Hall was owned by a sixty-member club of immigrants from Galicia, Spain, when we first began trying to buy the building in 1988. The organization, which was originally formed to help fellow Galicians integrate into American culture, had bought the building in 1970 and done very little to improve or even maintain it over their ownership . As far as we could tell, the group was filled with exceptionally small-minded people who really only cared about money .

Dealing with them for thirty years was like dealing with club schizophrenia. They reneged on their 1988 deal to sell the building to us and then made us dangle for fifteen years on a month-to-month lease. No matter how hard we tried to please them, there seemed to always be a major part of the group who was out to sabotage our family in some small—but nasty—way. If it was not snarky letters regarding a few late rent payments, then it was with threats of expulsion or demands for more rent to match other offers they had received—*after* we had reached a lease agreement.

Our success at Webster Hall ensured their success as well, and the group eventually grew to a thousand members. But not once did they thank us for paying three years of back taxes when we first arrived in New York City or for paying for their lawyers when they got into trouble with previous tenants, or for saving them from foreclosure when none of the group members wanted to provide any more funds for the effort.

Like all groups there were a few of them who where not so bad, but on the whole, I do not miss dealing with my longtime landlords.

THE HELLS ANGELS

The Hells Angels had a clubhouse only a few blocks from Webster Hall, and a motley crew was always hanging out there with their big noisy bikes, silly bandanas, and leather jackets. I bailed the Angels out of a huge problem with the police in 1993, but I don't think many of them ever knew that.

During the first year we were in business, the president of the Hells Angels beat up a group's road manager inside Webster Hall one Sunday night at the rock 'n' roll ball we hosted in October 1993. He managed to get access to this road manager by pretending to be the promoter's bodyguard. I paid the victim $10,000 on the spot to not call the police.

Although I don't know whether the Angels knew how I had helped them with that problem, we became neighborly early in our Webster Hall days. The Angels even helped us to fill the ceiling with insulation to help contain our noise to fend off neighborhood complaints. So I'll give the Angels a pass here, but we understood that with these guys you should never let your left hand know what your right hand is doing.

THE NOTORIOUS CLUB KIDS

When long lines of people started forming nightly shortly after we opened Webster Hall in 1992, we gained plenty of positive press attention and managed to secure bookings for some of the most prestigious events of the day. Our success was not always applauded by other clubs in town, and we particularly drew the ire of Peter Gatien, who owned several prominent New York clubs, including the Tunnel, the Limelight, and the Palladium.

The self-proclaimed king of New York night clubs apparently began sending groups of his "club kids" to infiltrate our nightclub, and not in a good way. They would cause mischief and mayhem, including pulling the fire alarms, which would bring the police and fire department running through a club full of people.

So what did we do? We created our own group of anti-club kids to mitigate their presence, and started our own legendary network of gay of loyalists. In the balcony lounge area, we hosted the clubgoers who invented the "voguing" fad that swept the nation during Madonna's heyday. This makeup room was happening nightly, and its loyalists also helped when Madonna decided to host her legendary pajama party at Webster Hall in 1995.

The anti-club kids also helped create positive and diverse fashion statements. They lovingly welcomed transgender kids who, like themselves, craved to embrace their own existence and self worth, and helped push the whole world ahead. Many of these kids went on to great success and left a legacy of hope in the face of desperation.

OTHER GANGS

The Aryan Brotherhood, the Crips, the Bloods, Albanian death squads, Chinese street gangs, and—the toughest of them all—Afghan warlords all left their marks on us over the years. I can only say that when individuals belonging to these gangs were confronted quietly, patiently, and with all due respect, they realized we were eager to compromise— or at least mitigate further chaos. We co-existed with gangs like this by either paying them off or negotiating a treaty. The treaty usually involved Webster Hall securing its peace by promising to keep secrets about the groups or particular members of the groups hidden for life. And that's all I have to say about that.

THE BOWERY PRESENTS

Not a gang in the traditional sense of the word, but this group definitely fits my definition of a group of people willing to behave badly for profits. It caused us lots of problems over the years—and it grieves me a little bit to this day that these assholes ended up partly owning our beloved Webster Hall.

Our interactions with them started in 2004, when I was approached about using the Webster Hall Grand Ballroom as part of a plan to grow their music booking business and create what was called a "cradle to the grave" business plan. The plan was to start a rock 'n' roll act in a 250-seat New York club and then move them up to a 500-seat New York club as the artist became more popular. As that club sold out, the act would move to our 1,500-person ballroom.

I thought it was a good plan (I did not know at the time that they only booked white rock bands), and we joined as a small partner in what soon became known as The Bowery Presents. The plan worked well until 2006 when a new partner was introduced into the mix. The new partner wanted to turn Webster Hall into a bands-only business full time. But we still had a very successful late-night club business, and I wanted to keep that lucrative aspect of our business going. The Bowery group then did three things starting in 2007 that caused friction between us that was never really resolved.

1. In 2006, I began working on a deal for a building on 56th Street that became known to the world as Terminal 5. The original plan was for us to lease the 2,800-person capacity club and then partner with The Bowery Presents on the property. After I had spent $100,000 on negotiations and drawing up a lease, the new Bowery partner told me doing a deal for the Terminal 5 building just didn't make sense for them. Reluctantly, I then backed out of the Terminal 5 deal. Much to my dismay, The Bowery Presents then signed a new deal in 2007 with the same Terminal 5 landlord. The deal excluded us from participating because they said they didn't want to work with me. But I think it was because they didn't want to share money with us.

2. In 2009, two years after the Terminal 5 deal had split our friend-ship with the Bowery folks, my family and I were negotiating our new lease with our tough Webster Hall landlords. Somehow, The Bowery Presents got word of our pending deal and offered our landlord more money to lease our building than the amount we had verbally agreed to. To our landlord's credit, he called and told me The Bowery Presents team had just offered $30,000 per month than we had already agreed to. The Galician group told me we would be put out of the building we had leased for almost twenty years if we didn't match the offer from The Bowery Presents. Of course I caved—at a cost of an extra $360,000 per year. Thanks, guys.

3. When The Bowery Presents sold its business to the AEG conglom-erate for $40 million for 50 percent of its business in 2018, they refused to pay me my 5 percent share that I was due as a founding partner. To avoid court, I took a settlement of $300,000 and let them keep what should have been my share of $4 million. I didn't want go to court as I was already working on my own exit strategy for leaving Webster Hall, and I just wanted to put this "gang" in my rearview mirror.

I know this gang didn't really do anything illegal, and I know I should not have been surprised to run into this type of mean and greedy dealings in the music business. I even continued working with Bowery Presents until 2014, although I never got over how they had treated us. So I was none too happy when I found out they were going to be part owners of Webster Hall when we thought we were selling to another group entirely. You can read more about that in a later chapter.

My advice to any reader here is to not too overreact when you are confronted with these kinds of issues. Think clearly and carefully and always keep your eye on the game ball. And know in your heart that sometimes it's better to eat a shit sandwich and save your business than it is to fight purely for principle and pride.

THE MOST INSIDIOUS GANG OF ALL: AIDS

"Hi, Mr. Ballinger, it's Anthony's mom. . . . He's your lighting man?"

As I took this call in the Webster Hall office that early spring Sunday morning, I became very aware that I was speaking to a worried mother. We in the club's inner circle knew Anthony was not well, but he was doing his best to retain his dignity and hope, and we were doing our best to let him keep up his pretense. But I felt tears in my eyes as I traveled up to the lighting booth in the Grand Ballroom that morning to tell Anthony his mom had called and wanted him to call her back.

Anthony gave me a sad smile as he thanked me for the message. I nodded and smiled and walked back down the stairs. Within a month, Anthony was gone.

We in the club business lost so many friends who died far too young during the AIDS epidemic in the 1980s and early 1990s. There was so much sadness that was felt in so many places. From the first whispers of a strange new illness in the early 1980s until the semi-effective treatments were developed in the middle of the 1990s, it was one death after another in club land.

But I believe that this curse somehow had a silver lining. It was inspiring to watch the brave and proactive ways the LGBT communities battled this disease and fought for better healthcare and better treatments. Watching those battles also created a better understanding for many of us in straight society. We became ever more fully aware that our LGBT brothers, sisters, and friends were beautiful and unique humans. And we saw them come through the darkest days of the epidemic as powerful people who had much to teach the rest of us about living life well.

Long live all of us . . . no matter who we are . . . or who we love . . . or how we identify ourselves.

"To this day I still wear a fireman's sweater with my name on it that was given to me for doing our best on behalf of the citizens of New York after the horrible tragedy of 9/11."

CHAPTER 29

HELPING OURSELVES AND A TRAUMATIZED CITY RECOVER

In my opinion, the many thousands of people who perished in the terrorist attacks on the World Trade Center on September 11, 2001, did not die in vain. New York—and the entire world—were shocked to the core, and our shock made us better people. The world stopped that morning, and then everyone I knew came together in a way we had never done before that tragic event.

Our security staff included some young firefighters, and all of them perished that day while trying to save others. So, this tragedy was very personal to all of us at Webster Hall.

We opened the doors to Webster Hall that day to allow the shocked and dismayed a place to come and sit together. Many didn't speak at all. Others discussed how they could help other New Yorkers. We made no announcements, and no one asked us for anything, but not one of the hundreds of people who came into Webster Hall that awful day was turned away.

Even crime stopped for a day in the city. It seems everyone was thinking about the people who were lost and the families whose lives were

forever changed. From that day forward, New York City became a beacon to show the world how a city could recover from such a tragedy.

Webster Hall closed for four days because we were located less than
three miles from the World Trade Center complex and because we needed time to process what happened and decide what to do next. Looking
back, it was the right thing to do. And it was also the law. Nobody was
in the mood for fun in the aftermath of such monumental loss. In the
days and weeks and months after 9/11, people from all over the world
came to New York City to help in any way they could. Many more sent
their love, their money, and anything else they could spare to assist the
displaced and forlorn.

My family had fallen in love with the idea of New York City when we
were kids crowded around a one-channel, black-and-white television on
our farm in Canada. That was one of the reasons we had worked so hard
to open a club in New York and why we had worked so hard to make
Webster Hall the best club in the city.

Even so, when we came to New York, we were still Canadians. But on
9/11, we became New Yorkers.

We loved the diversity and challenges we saw in New York. We loved
how cosmopolitan it was, and we loved how you could find every race,
ethnicity, nationality, and subculture somewhere in this city. We also
loved how all these different groups seemed to get along just fine—
most of the time, anyway. In the New York we knew and loved, there
didn't seem to be a lot of divisions between black and white or Jew and
Muslim. And New Yorkers could be quite friendly as long as you followed the most important rule in the city: "Don't get in my way, who-
ever you are, I'm in a hurry. I gotta get somewhere or get something
important done."

After 9/11, our love for New York just grew. It was amazing to watch
this city rise from the ashes and return to its full glory. After the initial
shock of the attacks wore off and rebuilding work began in earnest, the
City boomed. Real estate prices soared, and our business exploded.

And I'm proud to think that our simple nightclub helped in a small
way to make the city's rebirth possible. The grief and trauma from 9/11

were profound, and no one in the city could escape the reminders of that awful day. Clearing away the rubble and rebuilding broken neighborhoods was difficult work. New Yorkers needed a place like Webster Hall where they could come and listen to music and share their stories and leave the stress behind for a few hours.

We are grateful that we had the chance to offer just such a place to this remarkable city in those very dark days.

THE VIEW FROM THE DJ BOOTH

"On that Tuesday morning when the planes hit the towers, the whole city fell silent." — SEAN SHARP

Written by Sean Sharp, a true hip-hop pioneer and one of the greatest and most influential hip-hop DJs in music history.

For the first time, I didn't want to be there at Webster Hall. My heart was heavy, my head was buzzing with thoughts about all those we had lost, and in my mind, I swore I could smell the buildings still smoldering just down the block. It was a random Friday in September 2001, and like the rest of the country, and the world, I was still in pain.

I can't recall if it was days or weeks after the eleventh, but the psychological wounds that arose out of the attack on the World Trade Center were still fresh. The fear was all-consuming. Would it ever be okay again? Who did this? Will they try again? There were so many questions and few answers, and I couldn't have been more unsettled.

I was moments away from taking the stage at Webster Hall as the resident hip-hop DJ. The world's most famous night club. Our nightly basement party had grown to be one of the most popular parties in the city. But after the horrible events of 9/11, would anyone even show up?

My journey at Webster Hall had begun five years earlier when my close college friend Smokey Fontaine got a call out of the blue to fill in for two nights at this iconic venue in their hip-hop room. We couldn't believe it! Up until that point we had been doing college parties in Connecticut and small lounges around the city. But Webster Hall was the big time. Smokey was the DJ, and I was his hype man.

I never wanted to be a DJ. I was the "serious" theater major, destined for Broadway and beyond. However, while hanging out in the booth with Smoke and acting as his emcee, I discovered a part of me that I never knew existed. In real life, I was an introvert, uncomfortable in my own skin and especially around big crowds. But standing next to Smokey in the booth while he manipulated turntables, I developed an alter-ego while rocking the mic and hyping up the crowds.

In those moments I became SEAN SHARP (yes, all capital letters). Correction, I became "SEAN LEWIS SHARP!" The name was the same as the one that I was born with, but this guy was different. This was a persona. SEAN was brash and unapologetic. His voice could convince a crowd to do his bidding at a moment's notice. "Make some Noise!"

We became an unstoppable musical duo. Smoke had the ability to take crowds on a magical sonic journey by blending popular hip-hop and reggae tracks with precision. So, when the chance to rock Webster Hall arose, it felt like just the opportunity we had been waiting for—the "big break," if you will.

To prepare for the gig, we stopped by the club the week beforehand to see what the vibes were like. We made our way down to the hip-hop room in the basement. The basement was referred to as the "Black Hole" and there was a single disco ball in the center of the room with red velvet curtains covering the walls and ceilings. At the time, smoking was still allowed indoors, so the smell of tobacco and the cloud of white smoke were thick.

The crowd was refreshingly diverse. There were people from multiple ethnicities partying together in harmony in the same space. The drinks were flowing from the bar and the right songs were being played. But for some reason, there was no energy. As we made our way to the back of the room, we saw the resident DJ sitting down on a barstool, smoking a cigarette. He seemed disinterested as he switched from song to song. Smoke turned to me with a knowing grin and said, "Oh, hell no."

The following week, when we showed up for our gig, we were on a mission. The plan was to bring nothing but heat. We wanted to engage the crowd by talking on the mic, but not too much. Let the songs breathe, but take no breaks in energy. Smokey delivered a rollercoaster ride of up-tempo classic hip-hop anthems, including Naughty by Nature and Salt-N-Pepa. He would then sprinkle in popular old school reggae and some of the newer hits with labels like Bad Boy. To be honest, the records we played weren't much different from the ones played in the room the week before. But a world of difference was apparent in our energy and passion.

At the end of our set, both drenched in sweat, Smokey and I looked at each other knowing that on this night we had done something special. The next week, Lon Ballinger offered Smokey the position as the new resident hip-hop DJ. Smokey accepted the offer and implored me to come along for the ride. I gladly accepted. The "Basement Party" was born and what was supposed to be a weekend gig with my buddy turned into a legendary twenty-year career.

Every Thursday, Friday, and Saturday night we would spin classic hip-hop anthems and reggae with the same energy as that first night. Slowly, I was evolving from just a hype man to spinning for Smokey while he ran to the bathroom.

As time progressed, Smokey was being asked to play house music sets upstairs in the Grand Ballroom, and I was covering for him alone more often in the basement. My mixing was mediocre at first, but I made up for my blending deficiencies with my vocal abilities and that positive energy we had branded. Even though this was a super club, the basement felt like its own little world. The room was sweltering hot and reminded me of the house parties I fell in love with in college.

Everyone felt familiar because those faces were there night after night, year after year. Over time, I honed my skills and improved tremendously. When Smokey was eventually offered the gig as a full-time house music DJ upstairs, I was asked to replace him as the hip-hop resident in the basement. At first, I declined the offer, but quickly reconsidered and took the job. My only condition was that I wanted to incorporate more of the underground hits that weren't being played on the radio with the classic reggae and hip-hop anthems.

Mixtapes were starting to gain prominence, and clubs like The Tunnel and Speed were offering a grimier version of hip-hop that was transforming the genre, and I wanted to introduce that energy into the basement. I also wanted to fuse more of the burgeoning new reggae sounds and "riddims" into my set. I was sure there was no way I could lose. I was sadly mistaken.

For the first two years at Webster Hall alongside Smokey, I can't remember a night when the room wasn't at least close to capacity of 300-plus people. But when I decided to make the switch to the harder sound, gradually the crowd began to get thinner and thinner. One night, I heard a girl who came almost every night exclaim to a friend, "I liked the old DJ better." Soon, the once jam-packed room only had a few people in it throughout the night.

I was sure I would soon be shown the door and replaced. To their credit, the Ballingers didn't fire me. Instead, they gave me a chance to continue to play the music I wanted to play. Their gamble paid off and slowly the room started to crowd once again. The old faces were replaced by new ones that would come week after week, bringing new friends with them all the while. Our room became so consistently packed that another hip-hop room was added upstairs. A brilliant DJ named Chase took over that room and we became fast friends.

One night, one of Chase's friends came down to my room and introduced himself. "Hey, I'm Chase's boy. Do you want me to get on the mic for you?" I heard this type of request on a nightly basis and my answer was always the same, "No." This time was different. There was something about this guy. I had never met him before, but he seemed familiar. "What's your name?"

"Dexter, but they call me DLO."

"Cool," I said as I handed him the mic with some trepidation. When DLO opened his mouth, it was like nothing I had ever heard before. The booming, rich tone of his voice can only be described as a gift from God. The crowd immediately fell in love with him and from that night on, he became my new musical partner.

DLO added a completely new dimension to the basement party. Not only was he a great hype man, but he was able to take the reggae vibe to a whole new stratosphere. We had people dancing on speakers, visitors from all over the world trying to learn the new dances that accompanied all the new reggae being played. In later years, the highlight of the night was when DLO would play a song called, *Crazy Hype* by Elephant Man. He would have everyone form a conga line and they would literally run out of the room, through the coat check next door, and back into the room again while doing the dance.

It was pure madness and of course not something one would expect to find in a super club like Webster Hall. But that's part of what made the basement party so special. We were given the freedom to create, entertain, and have fun on our own terms. There were people of all hues, religions, and economic statuses partying together with no judgment. Just a unified desire to get lost in the music of the moment. It felt like the party would never end.

But on that Tuesday morning when the plane hit the Twin Towers, the whole city fell silent. There was no bass rumbling out of car windows passing by my Washington Heights apartment, no children playing outside in the streets. The only sound I can remember was the roar of fighter jets flying overhead. The feeling was surreal. Could New York ever be the same again? Was this the day the music died?

On our first night back in Webster Hall, standing in the booth waiting for the night to begin, I reached into my vinyl crate and pulled out Stevie Wonder's *Love's in Need of Love Today*. I needed to hear that record in order to cleanse my soul and prepare myself to get through the night. Slowly a small group of people made their way into our room. They were hurting just like I was, and you could tell they just wanted to escape reality for a minute or two.

It was in that moment that I truly understood the healing power of music and my role as a DJ. No, I couldn't make people forget the war-zone outside these walls, but I could help them lose themselves in the sounds emanating from the speakers. I could help them dance, laugh, and even sometimes, fall in love.

On that night, I also understood the importance of Webster Hall. In New York, most clubs pride themselves on how many people they could keep out. They think that's what makes them trendy and exclusive. But the goal of Webster Hall was to bring people in. And that mission was so apparent and important on this first night back. We chose to celebrate life rather than the fear of death.

Over the fifteen years that followed that night, I was fortunate enough to experience many epic musical moments at Webster Hall. From releasing an album called the *Basement Tapes* to having one of the first live shows on Sirius Satellite Radio, my journey at Webster Hall was legendary.

DJ Shaka Sean, an extremely talented DJ from Queens, became another crucial part of our team, and we eventually got a chance to DJ hip-hop in the Grand Ballroom (also known as one of the most famous dance floors in the world). Playing for thousands of partygoers every Thursday on Ladies' Night was more than we ever even imagined. Alongside some of the biggest guest DJs in hip-hop radio, we opened for the likes of 50 Cent, Alicia Keys, Wu Tang Clan, and Nicki Minaj, to name a few.

The Ladies Night Thursdays eventually changed into "House Party," an event with different themed hip-hop parties on every floor. This event became the go-to weekly party in New York City for two years, featuring a plethora of talented DJs, and performers. Artists like Post Malone, Vic Mensa, French Montana, and many others had their breakthrough NYC moments right on that stage, and we not only got to witness it firsthand but also be a part of it. My time at Webster Hall was transformative. I got to watch musical history unfold right before my eyes and meet people that I'll cherish for the rest of my life.

I would like to say thank you to Lon and the Ballinger family for giving me the opportunity to shine; I will be forever grateful.

RUNNING THE SHOW: USING OLD-FASHIONED STRATEGIES AND NEW-FANGLED DEVICES TO STAY ON TOP FOR 25 YEARS

"Having six clubs under one roof meant we were able to feature a lot of acts and some of these acts were already big stars, and others became superstars with our help."

CHAPTER 30

HOW WE BROUGHT HIP-HOP AND EDM TO THE MAINSTREAM

It took a lot of planning and a lot of work to keep Webster Hall on top of the nightclub world for twenty-five years. We had to make a lot of decisions and rely on some trial-and-error methods over the years. Some of our moves were tremendously successful, while others didn't work out quite like we had planned. But we learned how to pick ourselves up when we got knocked down and how to adapt when the world seemed to change overnight. And we never changed our core commitment to the core component of our club: the music.

From the moment we opened on October 2, 1992, until we sold the venue in 2017, the Ballinger brothers used Webster Hall to spotlight multicultural, diverse creations from new and established artists across the musical spectrum. With six separate dance floors and live music stages under one roof—and later with an independent record label—we helped move hip-hop from the fringes to the mainstream and introduce EDM to the U.S.

Producing over 3,000 band and DJ shows a year, Webster Hall helped launch the careers of upstart artists like Lady Gaga, Adele, Green Day,

Ed Sheeran, Travis Scott, Nicki Minaj, Skrillex, Dead Mau5, Diplo, Avicii, Calvin Harris, Kendrick Lamar, Travis Scott, and so many, many more. Our unique club configuration allowed us to promote musical acts large and small and gave us a chance to feature new music trends and emerging talent before others in the music business even knew about them. New acts such as Halsey, Black Keys, or the Kings of Leon would start on one of our smaller stages and then move into our bigger rooms as their careers took off. Curating new music trends and spotting up-and-coming stars became Webster Hall's lifeblood.

In the early nineties, we became the first big club in America to embrace hip-hop when we began to feature new acts in the small basement room known as The Black Hole. At the time, hip-hop was still fighting for respect in the music world, which tended to marginalize the genre, but our club DJs had their ears to the musical ground and correctly predicted where this trend was going.

Led by my brother Buster and our resident club DJ Vanya, we created a hip-hop floor that quickly evolved into a massive success. Our black staff members, who made up about half of our workforce, helped direct this initiative, providing feedback and enthusiastic support for our efforts.

From the Black Hole, hip-hop grew until it became the dominant music force at Webster Hall, with artists playing to packed crowds in the Grand Ballroom. Many hip-hop artists started their road to superstardom at Webster, all hosted by Funkmaster Flex, the legendary hip-hop DJ on New York's radio station, Power 105, who always hosted our legendary Thursday night House Party.

Smokey Fontaine (who now leads Apple's App Store) and Sean Sharp (now the owner of a charter school in New Jersey) were our brilliant resident hip-hop DJs at Webster Hall for over twenty years, and both helped us create a diverse and inclusive musical agenda that just added to the Webster Hall legend.

Webster Hall also helped introduce EDM (Electronic Dance Music) to the U.S.—both at our club and through our Webster Hall Records label. After discovering the exciting European dance music sounds at the Cannes Music Conference in 1998, we went all in on this new music style, bringing in big-name talent and featuring them in our Grand Ballroom with superstar DJs from all over the world. We knew a musical revolution was coming at least five years before EDM became mainstream in the U.S. because we had been attending EDM conventions and conferences and charting the sales on our influential Webster Hall Record label, where we sold over 2 million electronic and trance-driven CDs from 1997 to 2003.

In the early 2000s, we established Webster Hall as the foremost destination in New York City for EDM, bringing brilliant mixmasters to our world-famous dance floor. We were the ones who hired a couple of unknown DJs for $500 each: Skrillex and Dead Mau5 were just kids looking to get started in the music business when they came to Webster Hall, but it didn't take them long to establish themselves as world-famous performers in this up-and-coming musical genre.

EDM masters from all over the world came to our club for their first New York City shows, arriving nervous, anxious, and full of promise—and leaving us as certified international superstars. Just as we had helped establish hip-hop in the early 1990s, Webster Hall led America into the EDM culture, which helped it remain the country's most popular dance club until the day we sold it in 2017.

"Thanks in large part to our annual New Year's Eve treat, our Webster Hall club membership cards that let people get in to the club for free before midnight all year, we had a group of regulars who filled the place night after night and created that special warm feeling for tourists and other out-of-towners to enjoy."

CHAPTER 31

MARKETING AND PROMOTING FOR SUCCESS

Promoting a 3,000-person nightclub that needs to attract paying customers every night takes a special set of skills. Marketing and promoting are much easier, of course, when you have a fabulously popular location that is four floors of fun and great music. But keeping that business popular for twenty-five years requires imagination, a flair for the unexpected, and a willingness to try new things.

Ron Delsener, a famous New York City music promotor once told me I was his hero because I could attract people to Webster Hall with unknown DJs and roller-skating bears. He said we provided the "sizzle" while his bands provided the "steak." He was right about that. He told me, "You guys roll in cash, and I weigh the change." Quite frankly, New York had never met anyone like the Party Boys.

We learned to be our own promoters at our nightclubs in Canada, and we took to that concept like ducks to water. My radio ads were always quirky, inviting, and exciting. We created clubs full of lights, sounds, hideaway lounges, and mysterious anterooms and filled them with magicians, circus performers, costume contests, and go-go dancers—simple but provocative stuff that could only come from the minds of the hedonistic and mischievous.

In New York, Webster Hall itself was part of the promotion, with its world-class sound systems, spaceship-looking motorized lighting system, and other little touches that people talked about when they left after a night of dancing and partying. That word-of-mouth buzz is priceless promotional gold. But we never relied on word of mouth alone to keep the people coming.

In fact, we had multiple ways of attracting attention to Webster Hall. We sent costumed performers into nearby tourist areas like Union Square and 42nd Street to offer free passes for admission or free drinks. We passed out Webster Hall merchandise, hyped special events, sold annual memberships, hosted big parties, and made sure we always offered great music and a good time. That's how we made Webster Hall into the city's hottest of hot spots for more than two decades.

Our typical club promotions were usually pretty basic, such as offering a major discount on admission or drinks up until a specific hour. But we also created some special events and contests that were popular with our crowds, including singles auctions and amateur burlesque contests. (You can read more about some of our special events and techniques in the bonus section at the end of this book.)

Of course, our weekly Ladies Nights were legendary, and our LGBT nights were also spectacular. Four times a year, we hosted Rick Sena's Alegria, a unique party that was also an over-the-top gay celebration that would attract people from all over the world. The gay culture taught us to embrace new music, unique fashion, and most of all, tolerance and respect. We felt privileged and honored to help host these extraordinary parties, which helped introduce Webster Hall to new potential clients. We also gained a new set of interested clients when we became one of the first big clubs in New York to embrace hip-hop, and our hip-hop nights and special events quickly became some of our most popular.

Membership cards truly were our magic dust—the reason we had customers lining up for two city blocks every weekend for twenty-five years. We sold the cards along with New Year's Eve tickets—for $150 you could get into our New Year's Eve bash *and* get free admission before midnight for the next year.

The word *free* is probably the most effective tool in the marketing and promotion toolkit, and we used it often. Distributing passes that allowed free entry before midnight and even hosting open bars before midnight helped us prime a club with 1,000 happy, laughing, dancing people, ensuring the late-night tourists and rich locals would be met with a flash of happiness when they arrived.

So, on any given night, we might have 1,000 people in the club who got in for free and might have been drinking for free. They loved us unconditionally in the process. Then we would get 2,000 people paying full cover charges of $30 or more, plus full price for their drinks. This late crowd was the group that kept us financially viable. It was just a different variation on the loss-leader lesson our dad had taught us way back when we were selling cigarettes from the smoke shop.

Although word of mouth was our favorite marketing method, we also knew that radio and TV could be quite effective when used right. A well-created radio ad allowed us to say exactly what we thought our customers would like to hear. We tickled their senses with events we thought would pique their curiosity or remind them of how much fun they had when they came to our club. And when social media came along, we focused on the volume of positive Tweets we could get rather than fretting (too much) about negative Yelp reviews.

We always took a hands-on approach to promotion because we didn't want strangers deciding who our audience should be or telling us one of our ideas was too crazy or over-the-top. We knew who we wanted to show up at Webster Hall, and we knew how we could find them and how we could impress, inspire, and impact them when they got there. And we were confident that if they had a great time, they would come again and bring their friends to see the magic that was Webster Hall.

Our strategy paid off handsomely, like we knew it would, because we did it our way.

"Some people talk and talk and you never remember a word they say, and another person says five words that change the course of your life forever. Listen closely to everyone so you don't miss the good stuff."

CHAPTER 32

THE FUTURE WAS NOW

"It's going to become a paperless society, Mr. Ballinger."

I always regarded myself as a good listener. So when the young man with the crew cut waylaid me outside of my first-floor office at 2 a.m., I stopped and listened to his ideas about the internet and a paperless society.

"What's the internet?" I asked.

The young customer did not laugh or grow impatient with my ignorance. It was obvious he had an idea that he wanted to share with me. I discovered his name was Lawrence, that he was only twenty-two, and that he was an electrician. He was also a happy client who had obviously downed a few drinks to work up the courage to approach me at the greatest party on earth. It was November 1992, just a month after we got Webster Hall opened—and we were busy.

"It's coming, and it's going to be huge," he said. "It's going to change the way we live in this world. Everybody is going to be online, so that's how you'll have to market your club."

And, of course, he wanted to tell me how he could help—for a price.

"I have a hairdresser, a clothing store, and a fruit market that I've created websites for, and I'd like to create a website for you."

"A website? What is that?"

Again, the young man didn't talk down to me or make fun of me; he just said it was a brand-new technology that would allow everyone with a computer to link together to share information. He said the revolution was coming whether we were ready or not. We were not.

I met with the Lawrence the electrician/web designer the next week, after he finished working his shift down on the Jersey Shore. He stepped into my little office and used one of our huge office computers to show me what a website was. What I saw that evening was rudimentary compared with what you can find on the most basic websites today. But the idea that we could flash messages, provide sound, and use backdrops on this thing called a website thrilled me to death.

Lawrence wanted $90 a month to build a website for Webster Hall—I think it might have been the very first website for any nightclub in the world. The historic part didn't impress me much, but I was excited about the possibility of selling tickets to the club on this thing. With the World Wide Web, ticket selling was placed in the hands of anyone who could create their own website, and we were, "Lonny on the spot" in that department too.

Our "home page" should include several categories of information, Lawrence said: who we were, what we were, a chat room to discuss events, and a ticket download site. Thanks to that 2 a.m. conversation with a brash young electrician, Webster Hall became the first nightclub to offer discounted tickets online.

Two years later, the behemoth Ticketmaster octopus found out I was using my own website to sell our New Year's Eve tickets. That's when I received a nasty phone call from one of the Ticketmaster people telling me they "owned" the ticket business on the internet. Ticketmaster had almost completely cornered the paper-ticket market at that time, forcing customers to stand in line at their shopping mall kiosks to buy access to concerts, nightclubs, and sports games.

That dinosaur was dying, and I knew it. I also knew Ticketmaster didn't own the internet, and I was certainly not going to let them bluff me into surrendering our new online ticket service. Ticketmaster had created so many rules that benefitted only them, including sitting on all the collected ticket money and not paying venues for six weeks or more while they waited for customers to challenge ticket purchases.

Selling Webster Hall tickets through my own website meant we got all the ticket money immediately and became the masters of our own destiny. Of course, the online revolution would eventually change so much more than just our ticket-selling business. Many of the changes would prove beneficial to the club business. Many others would not be.

"Lon, why are you showing so much porn on your website?" I was gobsmacked by the question from the mother of one of my children's school friends. I had no idea what she was talking about, but I told her I would investigate and find out. The next morning at work, we opened what we thought was the Webster Hall website to find a collection of pornographic images.

Now you must remember, this was 1993, the very early days of the internet. It was pretty much open season and every man for himself. It turned out that a smart-aleck thief who owned a swinger's club on the west side of town had bought the domain WebsterHall.com because we had not paid the $70 fee to register it. We had not registered it because we had not known we needed to register it!

At the time, the internet was being used by less than 2 percent of the population and there was no body of government or authority to turn to for help. Opportunists had also registered domain names for Madonna, United Airlines, Bank of America, and so many other businesses and celebrities. This would come to be known as cybersquatting.

We contacted the porn-loving owner of WebsterHall.com, who had also bought up the domains for a number of other legitimate business-es, and asked nicely if he would give it back. He would—for the small fee of $30,000.

In my mind, this man was a lowlife who had no moral right to prac-tice such extortion under such a cloud of shame, so I asked a young almost-lawyer if he could intervene in the case. Richard Pawelcyk was working for us as a rock promoter while he finished his law degree, and he agreed to work on getting our domain name back. We sued the current domain owner and also the company in charge of domain registrations, but it turned out to be a long, drawn-out affair.

So for the next two years, we had to operate our new website as a confusing Webster-Hall.com and hope that everyone who forgot to add the hyphen to the domain name would not hold us accountable for what they found. Eventually, our case was used by the now stronger government authorities to demonstrate how charlatans were using domain names to run what amounted to blackmail schemes against legitimate individuals and businesses. The authorities overwhelmingly decided in favor of us, and the cybersquatting thief was forced to take down his pornographic images and return our domain name. The ruling would have allowed us to sue for damages to our business, but we never did because suing him would have cost us more money and more negative energy. We just wanted our name back.

By this time, the World Wide Web was booming, and everyone was expected to have a website. Online life was creating a new reality for many parts of society, and it spelled trouble for the nightclub industry. The Millennial generation started questioning what they were paying for when they handed us $30 to get in the door. They wanted more, and we had to find out what "more" was or risk being left behind. That dilemma aided our decision to launch Webster Hall Records—a move that helped us stay relevant for much of the next decade.

CHAPTER 33

EXTENDING OUR BRAND WITH WEBSTER HALL RECORDS

Webster Hall Records was our attempt to boost our club's profile while also trying to stay current in a music industry that was being challenged to adapt to a rapidly changing, more agile digital world.

We first set out to mimic Rao's, the famous Harlem Italian restaurant that had begun bottling and selling its spaghetti sauce in supermarkets. If we could package dance mix CDs and sell them to record stores, we reasoned, we could help Webster Hall's profile remain prominent and popular.

In 1996 I had heard that a London nightclub, The Ministry of Sound, was producing dance music house CDs created by London's local club DJs. So I jumped on a plane to London and made an appointment to visit the owners and managers at this swinging hot spot.

I toured the club, which I thought was just okay, but I could clearly see they were onto something big with the CD idea. I came away with a wonderful sense of purpose and great ideas for how we could also create our own dance music CDs for Webster Hall. Like everything in my life,

I was all in. However, I didn't have a clue as to how to get started.

When the Ballinger brothers decided to jump into the record business in 1997 we were facing long odds and a lot of closed doors. The recording business in America at that point was pretty much a closed-door affair. Record label executives were known as powerful and exclusive for good reason. They owned everything—the artists and their music, the CD pressing plants, and exclusive distribution rights to the record stores, which were basically more corporate monoliths.

But things were about to change in the industry in a way that would—initially at least—be in our favor. In 1997 the record labels had no idea of the shitstorm that was that was coming for them. In less than a decade, they were going to lose their power to select who would be the next musical superstars or how music would be produced or shared. The internet was going to change all the rules. Those of us with our ears to the ground knew big changes were on the horizon—even though we could never have predicted how completely the music industry would be upended.

I went back to New York City with a plan to establish Webster Hall Records and make it into a musical superstar. We would do everything ourselves. How hard could it be?

Of course, these were just big ideas without a concrete plan. What did I know about making records and creating a demand for them? Because there was no dance club industry or record labels to speak of, we had no roads to follow. We had to make our own roads.

The first thing we did was purchase thousands of dollars of advertising on Z–100, a popular radio station in New York and New Jersey. That's where I met Sean Megarr, a personable, twenty-five-year-old, salesman full of can-do energy and a genuine gift of gab. One day I took him to lunch and told him what I'd witnessed in London and my plan of adding "recording executives" to Webster Hall's resume.

The longer we talked, the more I sensed his excitement, and I hired him to help with Webster Hall Records. I hit the lottery with Sean. His relentless energy and sense of humor coupled with his exemplary work ethic helped me blow the doors off New York City. We also hired Tim

Bauman, a twenty-one-year-old with big ideas and a strong work ethic to help us.

Our plan was to become the dominant music label in New York City. Webster Hall was about to enter a completely new phase. Not only were people going to have a great place to meet, mingle and dance, but now they were going to be able to play our dance music in their cars, homes, college dorm rooms, and anywhere else music was played.

Sean, Tim, and I knew we didn't have the deep pockets to pay radio stations to play our CDs, like big record labels did, and we didn't have any distribution deals with the big record store chains. So we created a group of DJs, go-go dancers, and hype people to travel to college campuses to play—and sell—the CDs we created. And soon, Webster Hall Records dominated the Billboard dance charts. We introduced hardcore German techno and trance to a hungry nation, and we sold millions upon millions of dance CDs—each with a free pass to come to the club. This kept Webster Hall—the club—visible and relevant for young people.

We also targeted the young clerks who worked in record stores, specifically those in New York City, Boston, Philadelphia, and Miami, and encouraged them to stock our CDs. Every Friday night, we created a dance party in our balcony lounge at Webster Hall with free admission, free drinks, and swag for all record store employees. We invited every manager and all sales staff for all the record stores in New York City to join us for these Friday parties and to hear our new releases in person. Soon, we dominated all the store listening stations, and our posters were displayed on the huge front windows at most major record stores like Virgin Times Square. Within two years, led by the energy and passion of Sean and Tim, Webster Hall Records was selling millions of dollars' worth of CDs.

The height and popularity of Webster Hall Records lasted from around 1997 to 2003. Those were our golden years. Our music dominated the New York landscape as we introduced some unusual and never-to-be-forgotten talent and theme nights. We had great success with our New York dance CDs created with local DJ talents, including

John Suliga may he rest in peace) ; Smokey Fontaine (brilliant beyond words); Ricky Corbo (a lovely man who brought Latin beats into our music culture); and Sean Sharp (who created the unique basement tape hip-hop CDs).

We also brought in German DJs like the out-of-his-mind DJ Taucher, who blew away the crowd on the release of his CD masterpiece. No one had ever heard music like we played at Webster Hall on our "Tranzworld Fridays." Our bass was boss with its loud thumping low end layered with noises from flying pigs and upside-down milk cows braying melodiously with driving synthesizers. We took dance music to places no one in America even knew existed, and we were rewarded with huge audiences and multimillion-dollar CD sales.

It was during these times that we realized just how powerful the new DJ culture was becoming. We introduced the world to young Deadmau5, and a skinny DJ named Skrillex. The world of the big-name DJs was just being born, and we knew we were hitting the big time in this new frontier when up-and-coming artists like Dillon Francis, Tiësto, and Avicii played some of their earliest shows at Webster Hall. Our club and our record label were beginning to get serious attention from a brand-new musical world, and we were doing our best to understand the animal we had unleashed.

But no matter how fast we changed, the music landscape—and the whole analog world—was changing even faster.

"The internet and Napster changed the musical formulas forever. Cash disappeared from nightclub culture and the Millennial generation decided they wanted more for their money. People demanded unique experiences that overcame nightclub loyalties."

CHAPTER 34

DEALING WITH THE DEATH OF THE ANALOG CULTURE

While we were still trying to adapt to our newfound success with Webster Hall Records, a new world order was rising that didn't need records or CDs or tapes or anything more than an internet connection to get its tunes.

Young, digital-savvy music fans had let the cat out of the bag. You didn't need to buy an $18 CD to listen to your favorite songs. You could download an audio file from a sharing application like Napster and pay virtually nothing. In the early 2000s music sharing around the world was in its infancy and there were almost no rules or laws to slow it down.

Webster Hall Records tried to adapt by creating a web portal named allcd595.com where we would sell a full dance CD online for $5.95, which was far less than the price of most retail CDs in those days. We felt that financial model could work for us because it eliminated distributor fees since it didn't have to be bought at a record store.

Webster Hall was never part of the corporate culture. We were small, independent, and took great pride in being able to turn on a dime. Like a motorboat sailing between huge ocean liners, we thought we would be able to see a big wave coming and slip out of its path. But we were just a drop in the ocean of chaos when the digital age swamped the music industry.

Although record labels and artists tried to rein in file sharing by invoking copyright laws or appealing to listeners' sense of justice and fair play, it was clear that the days of $18 CDs were over and they were never coming back. Downloading and sharing music files became the new norm for young people, who perceived their actions as a rebellion against a greedy industry. They were enjoying doing the exact opposite of what the adults were telling them to do, just to prove a point.

Record labels were moving from panic mode straight into lawsuit mode as store chains like Towers and Sam Goody's and Virgin closed stores and then disappeared into bankruptcy. The modern-day music business was about to begin.

I knew our little record label was just about over the day Metallica sued Napster for allowing its users to pirate their work. This "new world order" in the music industry resulted in some dramatic changes for Webster Hall as well.

Between 1997 and 2002, we created over forty mix CDs, eight volumes of classic New York house music and dance mixes, and nine volumes of trance music. The series sold nearly two million copies with most bought in record stores in the Northeast. The CD sales added to our revenues while also serving as a promotional bonanza for the club. In each of the mix CDs we sold, we included a free pass to Webster Hall (if passholders entered before midnight). That offer added 1,000 people a week to our club for many years.

But CD sales came to an abrupt halt with the advent of Napster and file sharing. The internet changed the way music was sold and replaced the need to buy CDs in retail stores—or anywhere at all!

We tried to prolong the life of our CD business by creating the Umix-it format, which embedded a cakewalk mixing board right onto a physical CD, allowing the user to isolate music tracks so they could listen to the bass, piano, vocals, and drums separately. It would work great for anyone learning an instrument or for karaoke or for anyone who wanted to mix their own music. The possibilities were endless. We figured listeners would love this feature and talked Aerosmith and Billy Joel into using the format on their CDs.

We celebrated when the Umixit technology won the Golden Wafer prize at the 2005 consumer electronics show in Las Vegas, thinking we had hit the motherlode. But sadly, the public was never as excited about this technology as we were, and it could not save our CD business.

We surrendered to the inevitable and stopped producing new CDs for Webster Hall Records. We were sad to see it go, but we knew that the record label had prolonged the life of our club and kept Webster Hall on the cutting edge—just like we had planned.

Toward the end of our amazing run as a dance club record label, we could see the writing on the wall. Selling CDs was another business that was quickly coming to an end with the internet and the philosophy of music sharing. But Webster Hall Records had not only allowed us to make millions of dollars, it had also given us time to adjust our operations at Webster Hall for the next changing of the guard in the nightclub business.

CHAPTER 35

FILLING OUR STAGES AND OUR DANCE FLOORS

By the early 2000s, it was clear that Webster Hall would not continue to thrive if it clung to its old ways. We could no longer count on packing the club if all we did was hire a journeyman DJ to play long sets in our big box with the four huge dance floors.

For most of the last half of the twentieth century, nightclubs had served as a place you could go to listen to music you couldn't find anywhere else. The internet changed that. You no longer had to stand in line in the pouring rain for two hours just to get to hear what the club DJ would stream in the packed-out basement room. Now, you could sit at home and find any kind of music imaginable through all the various streaming services.

The internet even changed the dating culture, as Match.com arrived on the scene in 1995, to be followed by multiple websites and apps created to make it easier to find a date or a mate. The World Wide Web was forcing nightclubs to change because the new millennium generation was less interested in coming to a club just to dance the night away. What they wanted was a unique music show, which led to the rise of superstar DJs.

Clubs could no longer count on poorly paid DJs who would lug in their boxes of CDs to play six-hour sets. New faces and a new industry were calling all the shots, and they had no problems taking the reins and boosting DJ superstars like Diplo and Tiesto to multimillionaire status.

Around 2004, as the musical landscape was changing, I was approached by Michael Swier, owner of the Bowery ballroom, who was looking for a large performance space to add to his growing live music club empire. He was a quiet, serious man, and I felt he was honest. He and others, including his booking helper, John Moore, had decided to create The Bowery Presents. They wanted to challenge the corporate music brands like Live Nation and AEG for brand supremacy in New York City—the number-one music city in the world.

I was surprised by the offer and excited by the possibilities. I knew Webster Hall needed to change its standard operating procedures, and Swier's offer would help us regularly stage performances by rising musical stars.

Swier wanted to create a "cradle to the grave" business plan, starting acts in small clubs and then moving them to bigger and bigger facilities as their popularity grew. He wanted to make Webster Hall's 1,500-person Grand Ballroom a stop in that progression. I thought it was a good plan, and I joined as a small partner and entered into a five-year booking arrangement with the Bowery Presents. We could certainly do with the extra income, and I liked their ideas, so we bent over backward to help The Bowery Presents get traction.

The Bowery Presents would start young talents at its 200-seat Mercury Lounge, advance them into the 500-seat Bowery Ballroom, and then move them into the 1,500-seat Webster Hall. In addition to attracting enthusiastic audiences, this approach also earned us goodwill and undying loyalty from most of the musical acts that we helped promote.

Webster Hall and The Bowery Presents blew the doors off the live music business in New York City for a few years. But eventually, the differences between us began to cause friction, especially after Jim Glancy, the former president of Live Nation, joined the partnership.

The Bowery Presents did not like our wide range of diverse musical offerings; they were the self proclaimed kings of young rock n roll. They also were no fans of our diverse methodology or our loose methods of operation, or the way we embraced all cultures, or any of the other activities we created. Webster Hall booked hip-hop, Latin, rock, house, EDM, and more. Every musical artist who could draw a crowd was welcomed at Webster Hall, but The Bowery Presents only embraced rock 'n' roll through and through.

As The Bowery Presents partnership was crumbling, we decided to create a similar operation of our own, using our different rooms and many stages in Webster Hall to boost new artists from all musical genres as they grew in popularity. I called our club a "birthing hospital for new musicians," and we officially put the plan in place when we opened a 300-person capacity basement studio in 2007. My twenty-one-year-old son, Tom, was put in charge of the studio, which included its own entrances and exits, a VIP bar, a cool green room with an attached stage, and state-of-the-art sound, lights, and mixing boards.

A little later, we converted our first floor into the 600-person Marlin Room, setting up the next step in a band's progression toward the Grand Ballroom. Webster Hall's "birthing hospital" launched many a career in a variety of musical formats, and it helped the club thrive for as long as we owned it.

And the basement studio became our golden nugget. Ed Sheeran sang and played an acoustic guitar here while recording for a Sirius satellite radio show, and we hosted Green Day's Halloween party here, with Billie Joe Armstrong and his crew all dressed up in costume.

The studio became the gateway to the rest of our famous clubs' bigger stages, but it also attracted many huge acts who wanted to re-create their humble beginnings in small, low-ceilinged, rooms packed with sweaty and happy people, who were up close and in their faces. For most musicians, being loved and appreciated was more about sweat, silliness, and laughter than about the big and the extravagant.

The new owners of Webster Hall quickly closed these two smaller rooms while creating their own corporate and patented music hall business. What else could you expect from a corporation dedicated only to money? Nothing else really matters.

Section Seven

THE GOLDEN YEARS

CHAPTER 36

THE CHARACTERS

Let's be very clear by saying that many of the people who came through the doors of Webster Hall were characters, and that worked well for us because most of the people behind the doors of Webster Hall were characters, too. We embraced every misfit and minority group in New York City and were better off for doing it.

Because we then created a culture of happiness, coziness, and warmth where different and distinct groups of people could came together in friendship and bond over a love of camaraderie, music, and dance. From opening night, we welcomed and accepted the LGBTQ community and so many other characters and communities. All sorts of groups embraced Webster Hall as a safe house and a second home.

The characters on both sides of the club doors bonded in a forum of respect, inclusion, and support. We enjoyed each other and were inspired by each other, and we all thrived together. Webster Hall got its character from the dyke parties; the legendary super decorated all night Alegria, Rick Sena's unique party that was also an over-the-top gay celebration; the Bears; the Twinks; the urban Latinos; and, in fact, all the many unique or marginalized cultures that called New York City their home.

At Webster Hall, we focused on the universal right to dance. How you danced and whatever beat you found in your brain to dance to, we supported it. Our nonjudgmental nature helped us create and support such a fun, warm, diverse, and colorful culture at Webster Hall. And our grateful patrons were happy to offer us loyal support in return.

THE REGULARS

We cultivated a group of loyal and dedicated fans who for years came every weekend to dance and cavort in the four-story funhouse we had created on the dark edge of the East Village. Our regulars included Phantom-of-the-Opera-style dancers and an older Asian gentleman who shed his suit and loafers every Friday night as he morphed into a drag queen extraordinaire and danced the night away on the huge box speakers.

Latin Americans who enjoyed their very own music floor taught the rest of us how to really dance. The Fox and the Rabbit—a professional couple from Long Island—followed each other around all four floors, performing the cutest pantomimes of a fox and a rabbit all night long.

We encouraged people to express themselves.

THE GO-GO DANCERS

You would have a hard time finding a more eclectic and special group of men and women in various states of dress (and undress)—all dancing their hearts out—than Webster Hall's go-go dancers. We hired these dancers to serve as the undisputed cheerleaders of the dancing masses. They encouraged freedom of expression and passion for everyone in the club.

We would never have gained such affection and warmth for our club without the hard work and effort of these unique, bright, brave dancers. From the red, white, and blue bikinis they wore while performing under 10,000 balloons that rained down on President Clinton in 1996 to the fake twelve-inch penis that one daring dancer wore every night she danced topless, this group added so much heat that we never had to use the furnace when the club was full.

THE CIRCUS PERFORMERS

The circus performers were our secret weapon to creating excitement and a party atmosphere. Jugglers, stilt walkers, skilled acrobats, spectacular dancers and masterful sword swallowers amazed us all with their creative talents while prominently displaying the amazing Webster Hall family vibe. Their special skills on a high wire and sensuous cloud swings on a trapeze added an exciting dimension to every night in the club. Imagine the crowd's delight when tightrope walkers appeared out of nowhere, high above their heads, performing with no life support below.

THE FRONT-DOOR PERSONNEL

A beautiful, seven-foot tall drag queen. The four-foot star of the 1988 movie *Willow*. Famous wrestler Iron Sheik. Our front-door people were their own type of Webster Hall attraction. Seeing the variety of characters at our front door let you know you were about to experience something special and have a wonderful time full of mischief, music, and borderline madness. But although these characters set the tone for a certain crazy vibe, they were also serious, highly compensated professionals who helped keep out the ruffians with clear-headed bravery and sharp business acumen.

All good clubs have a brilliant front door staff. Our front door security personnel included men and women who were retired police captains, firefighters, and other huge humans—all dressed in black from head to toe. As many as fifteen of them waited patiently outside for everyone to see, and it was their job to help organize the human traffic that passed through our doors every night.

At the front door, we separated the unwelcome from the welcome and when we said, "I'm sorry you can't come in tonight," we meant it. The NYPD told us time and again that they advised smaller and more troublesome clubs—and other public assembly venues—to run their security functions the way Webster Hall did.

DRAG QUEENS

Webster Hall served as a kind of safe house for drag queens during the final golden years of the big time nightclubs and massive dance emporiums that dominated New York nightlife in the 1990s and 2000s. These venues were drenched in sexual vitality, musical passions, and outright inspiration, and gay black drag queens and transvestites (and Madonna) cultivated fashion and music that inspired this culture-changing time.

Even with all the characters roaming around Webster Hall, the drag queens stood out as they demonstrated their joy and embraced their uniqueness. We appreciated how they put our club on the world's playing field. Check out the incredible movie, *To Wong Foo*, the 1995 far-sighted movie that included a scene of a Drag Queen of the Year Contest filmed at Webster Hall. Thank you Baroness, Miss Understood, Jenatilia, and all you other beautiful souls who helped make Webster Hall so joyful. Long live the drag queens of New York.

LOSING SOME COLOR

New York City changed drastically after the 9/11 attacks on the World Trade Center. Before that tragedy, we had been leading a revival of the East Village and celebrating as it blossomed to life around Webster Hall. But the rebuilding and revival of the city after 9/11 accelerated the neighborhood renaissance dramatically. The entire world rallied around New York City at the time, creating a newfound interest in the city and opening up prime opportunities for the wealthy.

Real estate prices boomed, rents skyrocketed, and the colorful community that had made East Village so unique was displaced forever. Our clubs thrived anywhere we put them because we worked to become a part of the community. At Webster Hall, we embraced the colorful, the creative, and the misfits. These avant-garde, out-of-the-mainstream types instinctively recognized they had a kindred spirit with our family and could trust us. They offered us their passions, talents, and undying support because they knew we would embrace their differences.

Personally, I feel New York City lost a lot of its color when corporations and organizations like New York University and Disney took over the East Village and Times Square. For as long as we operated Webster Hall, we remained a throwback to the city's more colorful past, and we thrived because of our eclectic style—not in spite of it.

Under the Ballinger family and our wonderful staff, Webster Hall always recognized the rich, warm value of celebrating the forsaken and misunderstood—drag queens, dwarfs, transgender, white, black, Hispanic rich, poor, old, or young. We welcomed them all to the party.

WEBSTER HALL STAFF EXTRAORDINAIRE

Most were superstar employees, and many stayed with Webster Hall for decades. Although there are too many to honor individually, you know who you are.

And you know how much we respected you, liked you, and treated you fairly because none of you ever sued us. If we had problems, we talked them through, and we never had bad words with any of you. So many of you went on to such great things in your own lives

Thank you all, Webster family—from the bottom of our hearts.

"After meeting so many musicians, actors, and other famous sorts, you learn to leave them alone and recognize they didn't come to the club to see me .These hardworking, talented people came to put on an amazing show for their fans to enjoy. Our job was to help ensure their safety and that their performances went off without a hitch."

CHAPTER 37

THE VIPs

From the start we knew what we wanted when we went looking for a nightclub in New York City. We wanted a multilevel, no-frills building that had a rich history and would feel comfortable and homey instead of sleek and pretentious. We chose to be in East Village rather than some of the more upscale neighborhoods, and we wanted to create a club that would embrace the everyday, common person—and the uncommon ones who didn't fit in elsewhere.

Our goal was to be New York City's official nightclub, to claim that title for ourselves without telling anyone because we knew this plan would help Webster Hall remain a sustainable and successful venture that we could keep running forever. We didn't seek out the rich and famous or upscale because we knew they would all leave us the minute a new glitzier club opened up. Ironically, we ended up attracting a lot of that crowd specifically *because* we did not cater to them.

Prince said it best when he told the *New York Times* in 2005 that he had chosen to do his big CD release party at our club as he loved Webster Hall because it was not just for privileged people who thought they were better than everyone else.

We never clamored to get celebrities to come to Webster Hall (although we did slyly employ the legendary Baird Jones, Webster Hall's art curator who got our name mentioned in the *New York Post* gossip pages several times a month). Our ideal customer would be a person who would wait patiently in line, not object to a thorough search, gladly pay a cover charge to get in, have the time of their lives inside, and then go home and tell their friends it was the best party they had ever been to.

We didn't seek out celebrities, but we welcomed them along with everyone else. We never tattled on any celebrities to the press just for our benefit, and we never kissed anyone's butt to get celebrities to visit Webster Hall. The reality is that the entourages of famous celebrities are usually the main troublemakers in nightclubs.

However, we did work tirelessly to make sure the artists we hired to perform at Webster Hall got everything they needed or wanted. Sound, lights, sound booths, stages, and our famous green rooms—we knew how to help the artists shine when they were performing and how to relax when they weren't. Nothing fancy, but everything worked, and the drinks were always cold.

When musicians announced a performance at Webster Hall, they knew they would be playing in a friendly room filled with happy people. They could count on performing in front of 1,500 of their favorite friends, who knew every word and would sing along to each song.

We could tell we did our job well because we never heard a word of complaint from the performers who played at Webster Hall. We never asked performers for autographs or a signed poster. We thought of ourselves as their hosts and believed it was our jobs to serve them, and we got only kindness and respect in return.

After all, we weren't doing all this work for nothing. We were paid well, and performers would often relay thanks for providing such a warm and cordial facility. That was all the thanks we ever needed. It was just a cherry on the sundae when Pollstar selected us as Nightclub of the Year in 2016.

Although we never dished on celebrities just to get more publicity for Webster Hall, no book on our long nightclub careers could be complete without a few fun tales of some of the famous (and infamous) people we met along the way. The following yarns are spun from my memory and the memory of some of the people who worked with the logistics of booking, promoting, and hosting thousands of performers at Webster Hall.

DAN AYKROYD

Because Dan Aykroyd is a fellow Canadian who loves the nightlife, I've known him for many years. He got his start at Second City in Toronto, a premier comedy theater located in the heart of town. Danny (what I call him) was also a fan and frequent guest of our legendary Toronto clubs.

We reconnected in New York after we opened Webster Hall, and one summer Danny decided I was going to be his next best friend. I guess it made sense since we were both Canadians, married, and working in the entertainment business. Even though Danny always wore a suit, you never really knew what he might do from one moment to the next. But whatever he was doing that summer, I was going to be doing it with him.

Often he would bring his famous friends to Webster Hall to meet the Party Boys, and we would all enjoy the club's behind-the-scenes back rooms and dark corridors and just hang out and have fun. I got the sense he knew we were all basically just good old boys looking for a good time, and I think he enjoyed being out of the limelight when he was here, so we made sure to honor that. He once borrowed one of our other buildings so he and Tom Davis (a pal from *Saturday Night Live*) could collaborate on a comedy special for *SNL*. Danny is a brilliant comedian and a good man who brightened any room he ever walked into.

DAVID BOWIE

David was beyond legendary—he was mythical. He lived nearby so he often dropped into Webster Hall by himself to see new and amazing acts play. He asked that no one guard him as he preferred to not be noticed. David wanted to take in the show the same way as everyone else in the club. This made Bowie a perennial Webster Hall VIP—not just because he was a musical legend—but because he was a courteous and adoring fan of the acts we chose, the culture we created, and the discretion we provided.

It was at Webster Hall Bowie first heard Arcade Fire, before the Canadian group hit super stardom. Bowie ultimately collaborated, produced, and performed with the Grammy-winning band.

Of course, David Bowie wasn't the only celebrity who wanted to experience Webster Hall without any fanfare. We were very good at pampering and protecting superstars in sports, entertainment, and politics when required, but a surprisingly large number wanted freedom to experience our club and the world's finest performers in a more authentic way. We were very good at respecting those wishes as well.

MARIAH CAREY

Mariah Carey stood quietly on the stage in her glittering gown, her presence large enough to fill the giant ballroom. We were in awe of this beautiful American songbird, who had earlier been soaked to the skin while scampering here from the Virgin Records megastore in Union Square. Yet there was a loneliness and sadness about her that made you realize the price these super talents pay for the adulation they receive. She had risen from the legendary Sony records stables of musicians to become a shining jewel—of the manipulative music culture. I'll never forget watching Mariah's face as she stood all alone on the big stage waiting for her publicity ordeal to end. It was clear she just wanted to go home that night and leave the stress and hassle of the appearance to those of us who made our livings from her efforts.

BILL CLINTON

In 1996, President Clinton chose Webster Hall as the venue for his reelection party. He was at the height of his popularity at the time, and even we were a little star-struck that night. When the President came into the balcony lounge to meet my wife, children, and the rest of the Ballinger family, I noticed he shook the hand of everyone in that room—busboys, waiters, bartenders—no one was left out.

My mother, the infamous and normally unflappable Mrs. B, was so excited at the prospect of meeting President Clinton that she fainted. My brother Buster had to take her to the ER to make sure she would be okay. While he was away handling our mom's emergency, I noticed President Clinton hovering around Alex, my brother's very attractive wife. I chuckled when I realized the President was aware of her husband's absence.

Although no one else fainted, my mother wasn't the only one who was excited to see the President at Webster Hall. Everyone who was anyone wanted to be there—movie stars, rock stars, big-name politicians, socialites, the super wealthy, and our neighbors. This amazing event became the turning point in our relationship with our neighborhood. That night Webster Hall hosted the same thirty to forty neighbors who had been registering complaints about some aspect of the club or its crowds or its noise or whatever they found to complain about. But we welcomed them with open arms to hear the President's good word.

No matter what their political affiliations or their sentiments about politicians, our neighbors recognized the achievement in hosting the President. They knew that we must be a legitimate business run by stand-up people to be asked to celebrate this event at our club.

That party showed the world—and our world in the East Village— that we were for real. And it made an impression with the President, too, as Clinton's team praised it as the best political party they had ever seen.

HILLARY CLINTON

A few years after our hugely successful party for President Clinton, we hosted a fundraiser for his wife's run for the Senate. The two Clintons couldn't be more different. The President had been a warm, cheerful, and gregarious person who seemed happy to be at Webster Hall.

But Hillary seemed cold, aloof, and indifferent. I thought she was just going through the motions that night. She was the great female hope, but she didn't come across as approachable, inspiring, or likable, and the women I knew didn't warm to her. Still, I was pulling for her, and happy to see that she won that Senate seat. I'm sure she would have done a good job if she had been elected president in 2016.

JOHN DENVER

One winter night in 1995, I was flying from Toronto to New York and found myself seated next to singer John Denver. And when an ice storm caused our plane to be frozen on the tarmac for six hours, I had plenty of time to discover what a thoughtful and grateful human being he was. And I didn't come to this conclusion because of the booze; I reached it after hours of talking to him one on one. John was a warm and charismatic man who had the capacity to listen to others and make a person feel welcomed and appreciated. As if he was really listening to me or anyone else who was talking to him.

I even asked John how he wrote *Country Roads,* and he told me he was humming it to himself while driving his old pickup truck down a winding mountain road. When he got home, he picked a few notes on his guitar and had the song done in fifteen minutes.

He was one of the rare people who seemed to get what he wanted out of life. He told me he simply wanted to play his guitar, sing, and make everyone happy. I learned from John Denver that if you are lucky enough, you can turn your dreams into a reality just by putting one foot in front of the other. And of course, a lot of talent doesn't hurt either.

DMX AND RUFF RYDERS

DMX and the Ruff Ryders roared through the East Village to our famous Thursday night house party that my son Kaelin had created for Webster Hall. DMX (real name, Earl Simmons) came to the party with ten or eleven of his best friends. All equipped with giant motorcycles that they parked in front of our front doors. They marched right in, went straight up the stairs to the Grand Ballroom and directly to the big stage where Funkmaster Flex hosted Power 105.01 with superstar performers like Kendrick Lamar, Travis Scott, 50 Cent, Snoop Dogg, Nicki Minaj, and many others. Megastars all gathered here to commiserate, share stories, drink cocktails, and do whatever else superstar hip-hop performers do. DMX was a pure gentleman. He wished everyone only wellness. He was having a little fun on his night off, and everyone in the club recognized that. Even the biggest stars will show their true selves when fueled by liquor, lights, loud sounds, and beautiful people.

FAT JOE, OL' DIRTY BASTARD, AND PUFFY

It was the official afterparty for the Puerto Rican Day Festival around the year 2000, and the city was aglow with music, magic, and mischief. Fat Joe, the legendary Puerto Rican rapper and music maker was set to perform on our big stage when all mayhem suddenly broke loose in the big hall. We were at the mercy of the gods. Especially one big one named Fat Joe . . . Would we even be standing tomorrow? But Fat Joe grabbed the mic and gave a great speech to calm everyone down. It was unlike any speech I had ever heard.

Except for the one given in 1993 by Ol' Dirty Bastard from the Wu-Tang Clan who saved Webster Hall the night they played there. They just happened to be playing on the night that New York Mayor David Dinkins (whom I loved) was defeated by Rudy Giuliani. Ol' Dirty Bastard made a crazy powerful speech to stop a near riot in the big ballroom. When the record label executive refused to pay his $6,000 tab for the VIP open bar he had hosted, he told me, "You're lucky that's all you lost."

I remember one other speech that saved Webster Hall from some serious damage. It came from Sean "Puffy" Combs when he marched two opposing gangs out the doors of Webster Hall one warm summer night in 2004.

There is a reason these three men were leaders in their communities. They were wise and clever beyond the norm. People admired them not just for their talents, but also for their wisdom. Long live the masters of hip-hop.

JIMMY FALLON AND A GHOSTBUSTER

When you need a doorman who you gonna call? One wild night we were taken over by Doctor Ray Stantz (the *Ghostbuster* alter ego of Dan Akyroyd) and his honorable *Saturday Night Live* buddy Jimmy Fallon. The two decided they were going to be doormen one Ladies' Night.

They were funny and so full of personality!

Jimmy was checking IDs and frisking anyone he felt like frisking, all while cracking jokes and putting a smile on everyone's face—particularly the giggling young women. People often become spellbound when they come face to face with a celebrity, but everyone was so happy that night. Danny and Jimmy were both born with so much more personality than the average person, and watching their joyful interactions with our guests was a delight for me, too.

It's easy to see why the super famous actors, musicians, and other artists become so famous. I've found the great ones are the same people we see in the movies, on television, and on stage. It's not their talent to deliver scripted performances that is so appealing. It's their outrageousness, swagger, and confidence, which is evident in their art as well as their everyday lives.

BOBBY FLAY AND THE FOOD NETWORK

The year was 2000. Webster Hall and New York City were selected by the Food Network to host the cooking battle between Masaharu Morimoto and Bobby Flay. The two-hour extravaganza would determine which man would take home the title in the Iron Chefs Coming to America cooking series. The showdown, which aired on the Food Network, was filmed in our big ballroom.

The face-off came down to which chef could make the most delicious dish featuring king crab legs. Bobby Flay later said melting ice from around the crabs dripped on the floor and gave him an electric shock that threw him off his game. That's why he lost the challenge to Morimoto that day, he said.

The fact is that Flay didn't have the chops to beat Morimoto that day—or probably any other day for that matter—since he was known as a taco cook at the time. But the challenge drew big crowds and helped us spread goodwill and diversity to Japan and beyond. Plus, the Food Network paid us well for hosting the event.

LADY GAGA

"I can't believe I'm playing Webster Hall," the tiny little girl with the huge personality said to me one night as her mom and dad waited outside the green room above our stage.

Then she looked at me slyly and asked, "Do you want to know what I was doing last New Year's Eve?"

"Of course," I replied.

"Last New Year's Eve I was dancing on the top of a dive bar in the East Village pouring drinks down people's throats," she said. "Look at me now, I'm the headliner at Webster Hall." The charming performer was only twenty-three at the time and full of hope.

After spending so many years in the big club biz, I knew a superstar when I saw one, and Lady Gaga just radiated superstar. Her quiet, unassuming parents immodestly told me they had nothing to do with her great talent. "She came out of the womb dancing and singing," they said.

She was the complete talent for us that night, singing, strutting, dancing and leading her band through one new hit after another on her way to even greater heights of rock 'n' roll (and Hollywood) stardom. Lady Gaga was undoubtedly one of the greatest talents that ever graced our stage.

RUDY GIULIANI

We hosted a fundraiser for Rudy Giuliani when he was running for New York mayor in 1993. He was known as a New York prosecutor who was tough on crime, but he never busted Webster Hall for drugs, overcrowding, or some of the other crazy mayhem that he targeted in other clubs. I guess he knew we were careful, honest, and—in our own way—connected. So when he needed a place to launch his bid to become the mayor of New York City, we agreed. What I recall is Giuliani was a dark, sullen, hard-ass man. He never thanked us for our efforts in his behalf. He didn't thank anyone else for anything either, for that matter.

WHITNEY HOUSTON

Whitney Houston and her team created a video in our grand ballroom at Webster Hall that left a huge and positive impression on me—much as Adele did when she played on our stage years later. Both had a singing voice and a musical range that only comes along once or twice in a generation.

Whitney was one of those personalities I'll never forget. While making her music video with a group of amazing women, she was on top of her game for three long days of shooting. She was spellbinding, like the best always are. She had the most beautiful smile, and it never wavered through the duration of the video shoot. She was a hit.

What I remember most was the happy vibe she brought throughout the club as some of us got to witness one of the greatest singers of all time. I snuck looks at her from the balcony and watched her old dad sitting at the bar quietly watching her phenomenal performances. I was saddened beyond words upon her demise and wondered why nobody looked after her better.

MICK JAGGER

"What do you wanna hear?" Mick Jagger asked the six of us standing around the Webster Hall big stage back in 1993. We were awestruck as we watched the famous Rolling Stones lead singer rehearse for his *Wandering Spirit* solo concert and release party. It was going to be aired live from Webster Hall's Grand Ballroom and broadcast to America via satellite.

Even for guys who worked with celebrated musicians every night, getting this rare, behind-the-scenes view of someone on Jagger's level was an experience we knew we would never forget. When someone said *Jumpin' Jack Flash*, Jagger offered up a chorus or two of this great hit as he smiled and enjoyed our enthusiasm. He was first-class all the way.

Jagger rented Webster Hall during the day for three weeks and paid us handsomely for the use of our club. While he was there, Mick was the boss and everybody knew it. He would come in the afternoon to work on his songs after rehearsing yoga moves and dance techniques for three hours at another studio. (Don't ever forget that top musicians are also highly skilled athletes.) Wandering around the club to check on everything, Jagger was pleasant and kind to everyone.

During his rehearsals, Jagger seemed like a small, thin man, but the night of his show he wore a bright yellow butterfly style shirt over black tights and singlehandedly filled the entire stage with his presence. He looked like he was ten feet tall. Only a superstar could have transformed himself from boyish waif to gigantic music man as he strutted his Mick magic for all to see. He ripped through his new album and left us in awe.

ELLE KING

Elle King was one of the most naturally talented performers whose career we helped launch. With her mom by her side cheering her on, Elle had us all gather together for a group hug before she took the little stage and blew away the sold-out crowd with her *Ex's & Oh's* smash hit. It wasn't just her music that enchanted me, it was also her storytelling and wacky sense of humor (she is the daughter of actor and comedian Rob Schneider) that made me believe this blond force of nature was heading for stardom. Her multiple Grammy nominations have proved me right.

STEPHEN KING . . . AND BAND

The famous author stood all by himself in front of Webster Hall, reading the old marquee above the front entrance: "Stephen King and the Rock Bottom Remainders Live Tonight." I was mildly curious about his quasi-serious demeanor and his audacity to be just who he was with no pretension. There was Stephen King—Stephen King!—just standing there like any other citizen, alone and thoughtful.

Except of course he wasn't just anybody. He was one of the most popular authors in the country. I don't even remember why I was there so early myself, but finding him in front of our big building with nobody around gave me the opportunity to introduce myself.

"Hello, Mr. King, my name is Lon Ballinger. I'm one of the owners of Webster Hall and I just want to say what an honor it is for us to have you and your band here with us tonight." His band included other famous writers like Dave Barry, Amy Tan, Matt Groening, Kathi Kamen, and some others I can't recall. They were scheduled to play a fundraiser for a literary friend that night.

King was silent, but his face grew dark and ominous as he turned slowly and looked down on me. Without saying hello, King asked in a deep and very serious tone if I knew what was the problem with America. This was Stephen King, talking to me, and asking me a very serious question. Of course I wanted to give him a respectful answer, but I didn't really have one.

So I quietly said, "No, Mr. King, I don't know what the problem with America is."

Without missing a beat, he looked down upon me once again and said, "The problem with America is this: why would a band like mine be allowed to play on a stage like yours?"

I chuckled quietly at his sly sense of humor. Then he and I sauntered into the old building together, chatting and laughing like long-lost pals.

That night King and his cast of characters helped create one of the best and most fun-filled nights in the history of our grand ballroom, which had seen the likes of multiple famous writers, including F. Scott Fitzgerald and Man Ray, in its storied past. Long live the storytellers and merry makers.

JENNIFER LOPEZ, MARC ANTHONY, AND WWF

We hosted tons of movie openings and productions, but one that sticks out featured the two Latino stars who were married when the movie *El Cantante* was created at Webster Hall in the mid-2000s. The movie about the roots of salsa took several weeks at Webster Hall to shoot, so we got to see firsthand what these people have to endure to make a movie. We were not surprised when Lopez and Anthony got divorced, as the whole production looked shaky from the start.

Which is just the opposite of the Saturday Night Smackdowns that Vince McMahon brought into Webster Hall. The WWF was the most organized and professional production house we ever had the pleasure to host. It was fantastic beyond belief to see how a live production can be done so well.

MADONNA

To promote the release of her song *Bedtime Story,* Madonna hosted her legendary Pajama Party at Webster Hall in March 1995. She was amazing, beautiful, and sensuous beyond words. When we were introduced, I was most impressed by her tiny yet curvy structure, strong handshake, and confident demeanor. She was very much in charge of everything, and everyone in the building knew who the boss was.

During the show a few rowdy fans (and one in particular) wouldn't quiet down for the reading portion, but she got everyone on the same page quickly—with just a little help from us. We were honored she chose Webster Hall to host her eye-popping party and were not going to let anyone treat our guest poorly. The show was spectacular, and we got to learn firsthand just how someone becomes the queen of pop.

MOBY

I was introduced to Moby one night at the beginning of his career when I was invited by a booking agent in early 1993 to see him play at the old Metropolis Club at 18th Street and 4th Avenue. It was jarring to see only one thin man with horn-rimmed glasses on the stage in front of a wall of speakers and DJ equipment. When I arrived, Moby was playing the piano and simultaneously throwing his body into a handstand position.

He was a charismatic and driven human being who quickly reinforced my belief in the magic of humans—especially the gifted musical ones. We talked about him creating a Moby night at Webster Hall night because I knew his career was about to take off for the moon. Sadly, the show at Webster Hall never happened.

BILL MURRAY

"You're supposed to have $400 million in your bank, what's wrong with you?" I thought as Bill Murray fumed at me. Bill always came across as a guy who was worried about being shortchanged. He had come to Webster Hall in the early 2000s with Danny Ackroyd to see Phoenix, a band playing in the Grand Ballroom. One of the band members was dating Sofia Coppola, who was directing Murray in *Lost in Translation* at the time.

A fan took Murray's picture without his permission, and the actor went ballistic on me. I actually felt a little bit bad that the incident bothered him so much. On the other hand, Murray didn't give a damn if he hurt anyone's feelings. If there was something mean he wanted to say, he was going to say it. When he or other super celebrities put on a show, you are in the hands of a human tornado. If they want you to laugh, clap, cry, or gasp, they can make it happen. They can also use those same powers in other, less positive ways.

PRINCE

With all due respect to Lady Gaga and Madonna and so many others, the greatest talent to ever grace our stage was Prince. He simply was in a league of his own. I've met lots of great talents in the world, but—in my mind—there was Prince (and maybe Ray Charles) and then everyone else. He was that good.

I had the good fortune to meet this small but athletic man in 2005 and witness his show at Webster Hall. I had never seen a performance like it before, and I have never seen one like it since. Only 350 people were in the audience, as Prince wanted a small crowd. He also insisted that no smoking or drinking be allowed. Fortunately, he performed his musical magic before five television networks so others were able to see and hear it, too. But for the 350 of us lucky enough to see it live, the show, which included his eclectic thirty-five-piece orchestra, was like nothing any of us had ever seen. It was a night that only Prince could have pulled off.

A quartet of talented horn players followed Prince around the stage like he was the ranger in Yogi Bear's Jellystone Park. He would be playing some ragtime fusion, then he would shred his guitar with two beautiful female virtuoso guitarists, then switch to an old, beat up acoustic guitar and serenade the lucky crowd until they were ready to weep with joy. Undoubtedly it was an incredible performance by a man whose talents may never be matched in a hundred years.

Prince could have performed anywhere, but he said he played Webster Hall because we had the best stage in New York and because it was where the real New Yorkers went to party and because it was owned by real people. Long live the spirit of Prince!

JOEY RAMONE

Meeting and getting to know Joey Ramone in the last few years of his life was a personal highlight. When I first met Joey, he was in poor health, suffering from a form of cancer that would take this culture-changing hero from this world far too soon. Although his body was riddled with pain, we would often meet for lunch at Daniel's Basement Café on 10th Street. He would tell me about his early days in the music business and his times at CBGB, the club where the Ramones got their start. But he especially enjoyed reminiscing about how much he had enjoyed the old Ritz, which was now Webster Hall. We were always planning a reunion party that I knew would never happen. It was a privilege to know him and hear his stories.

KEITH RICHARDS AND RONNIE WOOD

We also hosted Ronnie Wood and Keith Richards who were known as the bad boys of rock 'n' roll. But when they were with us, these two Rollings Stones were just good-time boys having fun on the road together. We found that 98 percent of the many celebrities we hosted over our thirty years to be intelligent, charming, and helpful to a fault. Whatever you read about bad behavior is usually only wishful thinking driven by the negative press.

O.J. SIMPSON AND OTHERS

Any story that starts with O.J. Simpson, Richard Nixon, Elizabeth Taylor, and Liza Minnelli has got to grab your attention. We hosted an American Express party and fundraiser in 1993, and it attracted a wide range of characters, including Taylor and Minnelli. It also attracted two who at some point in their lives were (at the least) suspected of committing incredibly high-profile crimes.

When I met O.J. Simpson that night, he seemed charming and polite. Richard Nixon, who resigned as President amid the Watergate scandal, was suffering from phlebitis, making it hard for him to stand. So my mother, Mrs. B, graciously spent some time in our main office massaging Nixon's feet. Lucky for her, they were in the office when the wife of the president of American Express was on stage making disparaging remarks about Mexicans.

Despite the negative press generated by the insulting comment, the star-studded gala raised a lot of funds for AIDS research.

PATTI SMITH AND MICHAEL STIPE

Patti Smith was many things, including an important figure in the New York punk rock movement, a poet, painter, author, singer, and songwriter. Most of all she was the queen of storytelling. Patti's special friend (and our guest) Michael Stipe from R.E.M. was in the audience when she performed at Webster Hall on her birthday in 2015.

Patti put on her usual angst-driven show filled with despair but also with hope. We all watched in joy and peace as Smith entertained the packed crowd until the stroke of midnight when we dropped 5,000 balloons on her and her band. Michael Stipe brought out a big beautiful birthday cake as the rapturous crowd sang *Happy Birthday* in as much unison as 1,500 people under the spell of alcohol could muster.

Michael led the singalong and then did something he had rarely done since his retirement from R.E.M. He sang four songs that left the crowd spellbound. When I thanked him later, he was humble and courteous. In my mind, this incident represents the commonality we all share. No matter what we achieve in life, basically we are all still just kids at the birthday party, hoping to celebrate with balloons, cake, and our favorite friends.

BRITNEY SPEARS AND KEVIN FEDERLINE

Britney first came to Webster hall some time in the early 2000s to host a Grammy nomination party. She looked happy, but a dippy irreverent look seemed to be plastered on her cute face as she floated around our Grand Ballroom.

Her husband, Kevin Federline, was later performing in that same ballroom when he got a call from Britney letting him know their marriage was over. Federline had drawn fewer than 300 people to his concert, which is not surprising for a man who really could not sing. I remember him standing on the big stage when he received the news that his marriage was over, and the look on his face said it all. I read that look as "My meal ticket is gone."

Federline was a gentleman and finished his set before he left the stage, but I believe he stopped performing for the public after that night. To his credit, he became the main caregiver for his and Britney's two young sons.

TO WONG FOO

To Wong Foo, Thanks for Everything! Julie Newmar was a brilliant movie about three New York City drag queens, played by Patrick Swayze, Wesley Snipes, and John Leguizamo, who embark on a road trip. The first major film to feature drag queens, it was filmed inside Webster Hall for three weeks in 1994, and the opening scene with a Drag Queen of the Year competition was shot entirely in our club.

Three of Hollywood's leading men dolled up in makeup and sequins parading around in our club's smoke and mirrors made for an amazing, carefree set. Of course we already employed the city's best drag queens, like Miss Understood, but everyone was happy to have this movie being created in our club. Of course, the movie was shot at a more tolerant time before social media and nasty chatter became our society's new normal. The closest we ever came to real drama during the production was when Patrick Swayze—typically a real gentleman—lost his temper with the ever-hounding press.

Robin Williams showed up at Webster Hall to film his cameo appearance, which just upped the fun. To top it all off, RuPaul descended from the ceiling on a sequined swing to join thirty, completely decked-out, dancing drag queens. It was a spectacle.

DONALD TRUMP AND *THE APPRENTICE*

Webster Hall was chosen by Donald Trump's team to be a part of *The Apprentice* during the final contest of the 2005 season. Our venue was pitted against the Chelsea Piers, a sports and entertainment complex on the West Side. Our contestant won in part because we held his hand and helped guide him through his task to create a videogame festival. Donald Trump showed up and paid us in full for our rental, but that wasn't the first or last time he was in Webster Hall.

"The Donald" was trying to upgrade his image from Queens developer's son to Manhattan gossip creator when we arrived at Webster Hall in the late eighties. When Webster Hall hosted events and special parties, Trump and his family and friends were on us like a cheap suit.

When we first opened our doors, many big-shot New Yorkers initially thought we were the second coming of Studio 54. Of course, Webster Hall was a product of the unique Ballinger family, and our unique style included our willingness to tell everyone and anyone that we expect you to wait your turn and not do anything stupid. Obviously, as the world can guess now, that attitude didn't exactly go over well with Donald Trump, so he mostly abandoned Webster Hall as he traveled on to world domination.

"The Donald" was always polite to us and our staff, but you always felt the shoe could drop at any time.

STEVEN TYLER

Steven Tyler was our Umixit spokesman when Webster Hall Records was trying to save the entire CD business in 2004. Umixit was a technology that would allow CD listeners to isolate individual musical instruments and voices so they could listen to just the bass or the piano or drums tracks. Unfortunately, it bombed, even though it was selected as the winner of the Golden Wafer Award for Best New Technology in 2005. No one seemed the least bit interested in isolating music tracks—no one but Steven Tyler.

Tyler was brilliant and riveting as a spokesperson. I wasn't thrilled about having to pay $2,000 to send his hair stylist to the consumer and electronic show. But Tyler was another of those can-never-truly-describe characters who helped create the magical aura around Webster Hall, the same aura that kept us relevant for decades.

MARK WAHLBERG

What goes up always seems to come down and that's exactly what happened the night "Marky Mark" (as he was known back then) graced our club with his presence not long after our 1992 opening. We had learned about a recent disturbance in a nearby club and knew a person had been injured outside of that club at the hands of a bully. The culprit had not been found, but there were suspicions about Marky Mark and his crowd because Wahlberg had already established a "tough guy" reputation for himself in his hometown of Boston.

So our security was on the alert the following weekend when Wahlberg and his gang came a-knocking—with the press following close behind. We allowed them in, of course, and our suspicions were soon confirmed. Marky was a handful. It wasn't long before he and his troupe were asked in no uncertain terms to leave. That's when the screaming and yelling started as we forced them down the stairs and out the doors, but not before all our people had been "motherfuckered" to death. The press was Johnny-on-the-spot as usual.

It doesn't take long in this business to realize that many people nurture a petulant child in their soul, and they love to unleash that child for their own entertainment or for the entertainment of others.

KANYE WEST AND KIM KARDASHIAN

Our last big hullabaloo before we sold Webster Hall was precipitated by the massive rainstorms that closed the final night of outdoor performances of the Governors Ball in the summer of 2016. Kanye West, who had been scheduled to play that night, decided to throw a big party at Webster Hall and bring his then-wife, Kim Kardashian. We agreed to host this impromptu event and made sure to notify the local police precinct, thinking this could be big. We just didn't know how big.

As the night approached, the rain stopped and the skies cleared, but a different storm was brewing. At least 30,000 kids descended on Webster Hall—far exceeding our capacity. Pandemonium ensued. Cars were trashed as kids climbed on them, hoping to catch a glimpse of that year's reigning celebrity giants, Kanye and Kim. The cops closed surrounding streets, which stranded thousands in the narrow 11th Street corridor in front of Webster Hall with little to no hope of meeting the two celebrities.

At this point we realized we were not going to be able to open for the show. And we were deeply worried about what would happen when we had to tell the crowds that the show had been canceled. Somehow, we got Kanye to realize our impossible situation, and he began asking his followers to please disperse while the police valiantly tried to prevent injuries—or worse. And they did.

That night again proved that not even Kanye West can beat the New York Police Department at their game.

HONORABLE MENTIONS

One amazing night The Flaming Lips told the crowd, "We could have played anywhere in New York, but Webster Hall is our favorite place of all." Green Day never missed an opportunity to play in our club, and their unique Halloween performance (they all dressed up in costume) was one of the spookiest and best shows ever. When Ed Sheeran aired his show on Sirius Radio from our little basement studio, he enchanted the world as he played his acoustic guitar and sang his heart out while circling the room or balancing on a stool.

The Muse show was spectacular beyond belief. Lenny Kravitz stole every woman's heart in the Grand Ballroom. A young and shy Halsey played a show in our studio before blowing up and moving to the Grand Ballroom. She was always so thankful for the opportunity to perform at Webster Hall. The Killers would play for us any chance they could, same went for The Black Keys and the Kings of Leon.

We were every artists' dream club because we were cozy and secure and familiar and generous. When you worked for us at Webster Hall, it almost felt like you were hanging out with your favorite friends and relatives. Sadly, I'm afraid that loving and cozy vibe went with us when we left Webster Hall. The music behemoths who took over from us don't seem to value love and affection or understand what it means to musicians.

Everybody who was anybody came to Webster Hall and loved the warm family vibe we created. We gave respect to our performers and guests alike, and they offered us respect in return.

The moral of our story is that meeting and hosting celebrities at all levels from all art forms is not much different than meeting and hosting the thousands of customers who came to our club every night. In the moments when you meet famous people face to face, you realize they all fart and preen like the rest of us. So you just try your best to be who you are and chat a little bit if they seem to want to chat. But you are not their friend; you are a business associate. You both are there to do good work and then be on your way.

And that's the truth.

CHAPTER 38

LON'S TOP TEN MUSICAL ACTS DURING THE WEBSTER HALL ERA

I saw a lot of great acts and events in my decades at Webster Hall, too many to remember, from so many incredibly talented artists. But some do stand out in my memory just a little more because of their skills and personalities. Here are ten of my completely subjective favorites.

TOP LIVE ACTS TO PLAY WEBSTER HALL

1. Ray Charles, 1994. Ray was spectacular. He came to the afternoon sound check with Harry Belafonte, grinning and laughing. That night Charles played with a forty-piece orchestra and a nineteen-piece string section for the top 300 shareholders for General Electric. His fee was $40,000 that night, and because he had been ripped off so much in his career, he insisted he have his money before he went on stage. But then he put on a virtuoso performance that I rank either number one or number two with the next artist on my list.

2. Prince, 2005. The best ever. There was Prince and then there was everybody else. He came in with a thirty-five-piece orchestra to perform his new musicology album. There were 350 people in the audience for the performance, which was also being filmed by five TV networks. Although Prince would not allow anyone in the audience to smoke or drink, his royal purpleness left everyone in the house spellbound. He could not have provided more variety, skill, or athleticism than he did that night. The extent of his virtuosity was incredible, and he insisted on playing Webster Hall, where all the real New Yorkers go. Four four-hundred-pound, horn-blowing, black men in spectacular historic tuxedos followed Prince around our big stage, and two stunning female guitarists shredded their guitars equally strong with the master. Prince was without a question the best musician I ever saw in my life.

3. Paul Simon, 2011. Paul Simon asked to create what became *Paul Simon—Live from Webster Hall* in June of that year. We were all tickled because he could have created this show anywhere but he chose our place because all the other great bands, especially the new ones, loved playing there. He came into the building with his band and accompanied by another genius, David Byrne, and they put on a show to remember, especially when Paul performed an acoustic version of the "Sounds of Silence" that will stick in a person's mind forever.

4. Lady Gaga, 2009. "You know where I was last New Year's Eve, Mister?" "No," I said. And she said cheekily to me, "I was dancing on the bar of a club in the East Village pouring drinks down everybody's throat, and here I am tonight headlining Webster Hall. I always dreamed I would play here." Lady Gaga told me this as we sat inside the Green Room as her mom and dad stood outside the doors. Her mom told me they had nothing to do with her talent because she came out of the womb dancing, laughing, and playing the piano. Her joy was palatable, and her talent was prodigious.

5. Rolling Stones, 1993. Well, what more can you say than what an amazing delight it was to host Mick Jagger's *Wandering Spirit* concert in 1993. The prancing genius was a sight to behold and was a master performer who dares the world. He was larger than life. When Keith Richards and Ronnie Wood came to play one night as the X-Pensive

Winos a year or two later, we knew Webster Hall had just won the rock 'n' roll trifecta.

6. Black Keys, 2009. "We once drove 800 miles for a show and only two people showed up," Patrick Carney told us one day not long after he and Dan Auerbach had sold out Webster Hall. By that time, they were well on their way to becoming one of the top rock bands in history. We were so proud to be even a small part of their journey to the stars.

7. Metallica, 2016. The best metal band in the world asked to perform in 2016, the year before we sold the club. Lars Ulrich, the drummer, had frequented Webster Hall in the early 90s with his wife to socialize and dance. Metallica rocked our club that night, and their *Live at Webster Hall* CD was amazing. They blew the doors off the club and left their very best with our adoring crowds.

8. Whitney Houston, 1994. Whitney's father sat at the bar in our Grand Ballroom's big dance floor while his daughter performed. She was truly the voice of our generation, and her talent, beauty, charm, and sweet disposition have never really left the spirits in my soul.

9. Tom Petty, 2016. "I don't want to talk with anybody or shake anyone's hand," Tom told our handler after he had been dropped off near Webster Hall. "I just want to play my music and then I want to leave." He wasn't mad, just matter of fact. We said, "Of course, Tom" and then we took this musical genius up our old stairways toward the Grand Ballroom on the fourth floor. At one point, Tom said, "If it's too much further, you may have to carry me." Of course everyone chuckled, but honestly he did not look great and you could tell he did not feel well. He passed away about eight months later, and news of his death made me sad but did not surprise me. Tom loved that show he performed in Webster Hall with his old band, Mudcrutch. I could tell by the kind, gentle smile on his face as he finished his encore while 1,500 fans clapped and stomped.

10. 2010 era. There were so many amazing performances in these years that I can't pick just one. We got to host and enjoy the Kings of Leon, The Black Keys, The Killers, Cage The Elephant, Usher, Halsey, Avril Lavigne, Leon Bridges, Wiz Khalifa, 50 Cent, Snoop Dogg, Sting,

Rihanna, and so many more incredible shows. They all put on such great concerts that felt so much more special than any festival or arena experience could. Bands came to Webster Hall because they felt the love, and I think the musicians were always at their best here because it was always like they were with their very best friends in the world.

BIGGEST AND BEST EVENTS AT WEBSTER HALL

1. Bill Clinton Presidential Announcement Party. This event in February of 1996 solidified our importance as the most diversified club in the neighborhood. And it eased all the problems we were having with the police and our local neighborhood to bed forever. Bill Clinton was so popular in New York City at this time that his event at Webster Hall became a public relations master stroke for our brand.

2. Madonna's Pajama Party and *Bedtime Story* Release, 1995. Madonna was so cool and sexy and a small, perfectly proportioned storyteller sharing her new album with us. I have wondered if she and Carlos Leon conceived Lourdes that night because she was born nine months later and Carlos was part of Madonna's dance team that night at Webster Hall. But, who cares? Madonna was awesome, and she has contributed so much to dance and music culture. We were so proud to host her incredible pajama party.

3. Opening Night, October 2 1992. I wrote a whole chapter about this night, but it still deserves to be in this list. I spent most of my life as a nightclub proprietor, and I have never seen a more profound and exotic opening than the one at Webster Hall. It was beyond anything you could have imagined in your wildest of dreams with 15,000 very cool people trying to get into our soon-to-be legendary, four-story, 40,000-square-foot funhouse full of circus acts, tarot card readers, naked go-go dancers, and even Anthony Kiedis from the Red Hot Chili Peppers doing cartwheels on the big dance floor. Then my wife, Lois, who had endured so much stress as we lost our home and our Canadian real estate portfolio, caught me by the arm and gave me a smile as tears of joy ran down her face.

4. Every New Year's Eve. They were all breathtaking. We hosted up to 12,000 people with our special twenty-four-hour liquor license, for twenty-five years, we offered the most meaningful place to celebrate the new year. We always billed the night as "the largest balloon drop in the history of the free world." Google Webster Hall New Year's Eve parties and see for yourself what crazy, happy times we all shared.

5. Every Halloween. They were all beyond spectacular. Webster Hall was always the afterparty for the notorious West Village Halloween parades. The entire place was decked out in cobwebs and black tunnels and so many decorations, and our $5,000 costume contest attracted the most incredible costumes. Halloween was our night. Webster Hall owned Halloween nights in New York City, and everyone wanted to be there.

Section Eight

THE END OF AN ERA

"We proved that our simple plan of diversity and respect for most everyone we encountered, coupled with our dedication and hard work, were really unbeatable. Thanks, Mom."

CHAPTER 39

OPENING OUR WINDOW OF OPPORTUNITY!

In business (and in life), it's important to recognize when you are presented with a golden opportunity. Ideal moments to make great changes in your life don't come often, and they don't stick around long either. Recognizing those opportune moments and either moving forward or choosing to let the opportunity pass could very possibly have a major impact on your life—and the lives of those who depend on you. The most important thing is to *choose*—even if you choose to stand still. Don't miss your chance just because you can't make up your mind.

By the end of 2015, Webster Hall had reached dizzying heights of nightclub success. In that year, we had grossed $25 million and hosted 1.2 million people who enjoyed nearly 3,000 bands, DJs, comedians, and other performers within our walls.

More than two decades after we opened, we were still at the top of the nightclub game—in fact, a few months later, *Pollstar*, the music industry bible, would name Webster Hall the best nightclub in the world for the year 2016. But things in the industry were changing again. The big-money/big-power music conglomerates were making it harder and harder to book top acts into Webster Hall; liability insurance rates were skyrocketing, and profit margins were shrinking.

For years, we had been the envy of the music industry because of all the great artists who wanted to play at Webster Hall. We got Metallica, Muse, Paul Simon, Prince, Tom Petty, Madonna, Rolling Stones, and so many, many more who wanted to play at our diversified Webster Hall. For many of these well-established acts, it wasn't about the money. They just wanted to perform where the young hip acts played, and we were that place.

But money has a funny way of changing people's perspectives—and decisions. The beginning of the end for us started with the music festivals. The big boys had the deep pockets to run the Governor's Ball and other huge local music events. The bands that would normally play on our stages were offered six times the amount of money we could offer to play the festivals. *And* they had to agree not to play within a certain geographical radius for at least six months before and after the music festival. Because Webster Hall is in the heart of New York City, it was within the forbidden zone of lots of big festivals. That made it harder to fill our stages, especially during the busy summer months.

To make matter worse, as I mentioned, our liability insurance fees had skyrocketed while also becoming both more important and less useful. In the days of the MeToo movement, liability insurance was more than necessary in a business like ours. But we paid almost a million dollars per year for insurance for a policy that only allowed a million dollars for each individual claim—and carried a whopping $100,000 deductible for each claim.

Adding to our expenses were the rising costs of everything from staff wages to sound equipment. Our profit margins had slipped from around 15 percent when we first opened to less than 5 percent. The handwriting was on the wall. Independently operated music venues, especially in big cities, were on their way out.

Things in my personal life were changing, too. I had just welcomed Sage, our first grandchild, into the world, which was just another reminder that our three-brother original ownership team was getting older. I didn't ever want the club to lose its dominance just because we had hung on too long. I also had to think about the future of the younger people I relied on to help Webster Hall maintain its position as musical powerhouse. I knew what I wanted to do—and needed to do.

We had enough time left on our lease that I was confident we could attract a huge music corporation with big bucks to buy us. I also knew the players who would be interested in securing Webster Hall and believed we could get a lot of money for the venue at that time. It was truly our golden window of opportunity.

I contacted an investment bank in early 2016 and had a tentative agreement within two weeks to sell the venue for $45 million to a Russian oligarch and entertainment mogul. This offer was more than enough to guarantee me and my partners a nice retirement after forty years of hard work, and the deal would include our entire Webster Hall staff staying on to keep the business managed properly.

It was hard to leave the place where my family and I had poured out our blood, sweat, and tears for so many years. Especially because I felt we had the moxie and talent to keep Webster Hall going forever if we chose to.

But I also felt like this deal gave us the chance to walk out with our heads held high and our pockets full while caring for our loyal staff—instead of watching the greedy music corporations squeeze us to death by attrition.

Of course, the deal to sell Webster Hall wound up being a lot more complex than it initially appeared to be—just like every deal we had made since we first set our sights on the historic building. And those music sharks I had been trying to avoid would wind up getting a piece of my heart after all. But I'm still glad I saw my opportunity window and I opened it when I did.

"Well, you can't cry over disappointments forever."

CHAPTER 40

DEALING WITH THE SNEAKY RUSSIANS

The Russian oligarch who ambled into the club that summer day in 2017 was nearly seven feet tall and had a deep, booming voice. Mikhail Prokhorov got out of the black Cadillac Escalade (stereotypical car of all rich New Yorkers) and made his way into the building. As the owner of the Brooklyn Nets and the Barclays Center headed toward the music, I knew he would soon own Webster Hall, too, and we would be leaving. I needed to get used to the idea but still couldn't quite wrap my head around it.

Prokhorov slowly and politely walked the entire building. He gave no orders and made no demands. He just wanted to see this great American asset. By the time he finished his tour, he was giggling like a child because he knew Webster Hall was more than a building—it was a real New York City entertainment brand that had been forged out of the Ballinger family's know-how, imagination, ambition, and hard work.

Prokhorov had jumped on the chance to buy Webster Hall almost as soon as I floated the idea of selling it. He sent his advance team to see the venue, which they loved, and in April 2016, Prokhorov's Brooklyn

Sports and Entertainment (BSE) made a formal offer to buy Webster Hall for $45 million. Soon, his lawyers were meeting our lawyers to try to finalize the deal.

A year later, with the deal still not final, I finally discovered why. Seems that BSE had decided to split ownership of Webster Hall with AEG and The Bowery Presents, which had been recently bought by AEG. These new partners had plans to run the club that did not include the current Webster Hall management staff. They had never discussed that with me before and the news landed like a punch to my gut.

I had promised my staff for months that their jobs were not at risk. BSE said they respected and appreciated the way we ran the business, so I told my staff that BSE was looking forward to working with them. But now I was learning that the arrogant corporate music groups that I had feuded with for years would soon be controlling our beloved club and that my entire staff would be let go. It was extremely disappointing, to say the least.

Apparently, BSE had broken the nondisclosure agreement we signed in the beginning and had been working on this deal with AEG behind our back. Dragging out these purchase negotiations for so long had cost Webster Hall hundreds of thousands of dollars in unnecessary lawyer fees and left us in a state of low-level anxiety for months.

And what about my wonderful, loyal staff? Many of them had been with us for twenty years or more. How was I going to tell them the plans had been changed? And, oh, how I hated the thought of turning even part of our club over to The Bowery Presents. In addition to the shabby way they had always treated us over the years, their team booked only rock 'n' roll bands, while hip-hop and EDM were now the heart and soul of Webster Hall. Bowery Presents bought into the Jann Wenner *Rolling Stone* school of thought.

I was distraught and devastated, and I toyed with the idea of trying to stop the deal or suing BSE for breaching our NDA. But I soon realized our little independent business—even with our own team of high-priced lawyers—would not be able to overcome the firepower of BSE, AEG, and The Bowery Presents.

Ironically, the dirty dealing related to the sale just confirmed my gut feeling that it was time to go. There was no way to engage in a fair fight with the behemoth music corporations. We had enjoyed twenty-five years at the peak of the New York City club scene and had shared our dance floors and stages with all cultures and people from all walks of life. We could now leave while we were still at the top. The deal did not protect my management team or preserve our way of doing business the way I had hoped it would, but I did the best I could do.

Looking back, I choose not to focus on the disappointment of that final deal. I enjoyed the view from the best seat at the best club in the world for twenty-five years. How could I really complain?

I'm also proud to report that many of our wonderful Webster Hall staff went on to have amazing careers and are now the new leaders of the ever-changing music world.

"Opening, building, and maintaining the high standards Webster Hall represented was our Mount Everest. We had made it to the top—and we had remained there for twenty-five years. It was time to celebrate our incredible success and look for other mountains to climb."

CHAPTER 41

SO LONG, OLD GIRL. I'M SURE GOING TO MISS YOU

In the wee hours of August 17, 2017, after Skrillex's final performances at Ballinger-owned Webster Hall, I stood alone in the basement and let wonderful memories flow through me. I felt proud, grateful, and in awe of what we had created. Steve, Buster, and I had begun with little more than a vision, and we had made that vision a reality with the aid and support of the rest of our family and a loyal, loving, hard-working staff.

We had helped more than thirty million people laugh, dance, and lose themselves in music and an atmosphere of joy and adventure. Webster Hall had greased the wheels of countless romances and friendships while also boosting the careers of scores of musicians and DJs and other artists. We helped move hip-hop and EDM into the mainstream, embraced characters and cultures that had been shoved to the margins for too long, and sparked an East Village revival.

And, I liked to think, we had faithfully maintained and enhanced Webster Hall itself. What others saw as a building had always seemed more like a living a partner to me. She was sturdy and strong, predictable and reliable, beautiful but quirky. The Old Girl—as I liked to call her—had experienced a lot of history in her 131 years, and she was still ready to party.

I walked every inch of the building I had come to love so much and thanked her for all of her support and her loyalty, and what she had provided for me and my family over so many years. Starting in the sub-basement, I visited the little spot next to the weathered furnace where my cronies and I would slip away to puff on a little pot. Walking slowly and quietly, I made my way through the basement studio spaces and onto the first floor where we had rocked out for years. From there I ascended to the Grand Ballroom through the secret and extraordinary balcony lounge. I paused on the Grand Ballroom stage where so much magic happened.

As I climbed my way through the levels of Webster Hall, memories crowded my mind—special people, incredible shows, important events, outrageous celebrations, joyful laughs. This place and what happened here had all meant so much to me and my family. And what we did here had meant so much to New York and all of the people who passed through and were touched by this special place. Twenty-five years of challenges, hardships, dramas, successes, and hard work passed by in mere minutes.

I stepped out to the street and gazed at the old marquee that announced the "END OF AN ERA." How true that was.

Leaving Webster Hall that early morning was one of the hardest things I have ever done. I vacillated from the happiness triggered by all the great memories to sorrow for leaving a place that had been so intertwined with my life for so long.

I thanked the Old Girl and told her I was leaving and wouldn't be back because she wasn't mine anymore. I swear I felt her shudder. Two weeks after we finalized the deal and left for good, Webster Hall's new owners closed her up and started a massive indoor renovation project.

Apparently the indoor work destabilized the building enough to send the old marquee crashing down from the front of the building. Deep in my heart, I think it was just the Old Girl's way of saying she was going to miss us too.

Epilogue

MOVING ON

"We came. We saw. We conquered. And we left. We proved beyond any shadow of doubt that, indeed, nice guys can finish first in New York City, too. We may not have started off on great footing, but we ended up on top—just like in our little farm-kid dreams.

NO REGRETS

In March 2020, a novel coronavirus made its way to New York City and changed everything. Almost every indoor gathering spot was ordered to close, including nightclubs. As the closures stretched into weeks, then months, then years, I grew ever more grateful that we had sold Webster Hall in 2017.

I truly don't know whether we would have been able to outlast the COVID shutdowns. The Ballingers are survivors who don't give up easily and somehow always seem to land on our feet. But that savage worldwide shutdown could have easily crushed us too.

It had been incredibly hard for us to walk away from Webster Hall even though we were able to make a lucrative deal. When I saw the window of opportunity opening for us in 2016, I still had to make the gut-wrenching decision to "GO." We walked away from Webster Hall for the last time in August of 2017, and deep down I knew we had made the right decision. COVID removed every trace of doubt.

Webster Hall's new owners closed the club for almost two years while they made some major renovations to the building, adding elevators, expanding restrooms, and overhauling the sound system. They reopened Webster Hall with great fanfare in April 2019 but didn't even make it to their first anniversary before the COVID shutdowns. Good thing the new owners had pockets deep enough to survive that!

Narrowly missing the COVID shutdown mess reinforced my basic belief in acting on your good judgment and your instincts. If I had given in to my sentimental side and hung onto my beloved Webster Hall against all my better judgment, we would have been forced to endure the gut-wrenching pandemic with all its misery and unthinkable nightmares.

From our humble beginnings as scruffy Canadian farm boys, we always followed a central philosophy: do what you know is right for you and never look back and regret what you may have missed.

That principle had helped us rise from owners of a laundromat in a tiny corner of Canada to become some of the greatest nightclub operators in the world. The Ballinger brothers weathered nightclub storms together for nearly forty years, and we stood alone on top of the entertainment mountain in New York City for a quarter century.

Under our careful and creative watch, Webster Hall had been in a league of its own. We achieved such lasting success by being open and welcoming to everyone and anyone who wanted to come to listen, dance, and enjoy themselves. No matter who you where or how much money you had.

We were honored by the general public's love and affection for our nightclubs and our parties. We treasure the grace and appreciation we received from the New York and world press, the support we received from the police, the firefighters, and all the many music stars and bohemian entertainers we hosted over forty years. We learned to love and embrace all of our incredible staff members and to bask in their affections for us.

This incredible journey would not have been possible without you, dear readers. My family and I thank you from the bottom of our hearts for all of your loyalty and support.

Bonus Section 1

LON'S PRACTICAL ADVICE FOR RUNNING THE BEST BUSINESS IN YOUR WORLD

FORTY YEARS OF "ROUGH TRADE" WISDOM

I am often asked how we lasted so long in the cut-throat nightclub business when most operators failed after just a few years. In this bonus section, I share advice from my forty years in what is often called the "rough trade." It can be helpful for anyone who wants to build a successful hospitality business for the long haul. In fact, much of the advice I'm sharing can apply to almost any business venture.

It's worth noting that a lot of my advice is about what *not* to do. I hope readers will pay special attention to these stories of when things went south for us and how we failed forward, licked our wounds, learned our lessons, and came out on the other side smarter and stronger for having endured the tough times. We did all of this so you don't have to. That is, if you pay attention.

The nightclub and music industry is called the "rough trade" because it is so hard to succeed in this business and also because the type of people who gravitate toward it are often not very reputable . If you can make it in this business, you can make it in any business. After forty years of successes and failures, I recognize that nice guys can finish first, but only if you do the right thing—and do the right things right—and treat everyone—and I mean everyone—with respect. That is the only way you can rise to the top of a field known for misbehavior, selfishness, and greed. And the Ballinger family proves that you can not only rise to the top, but you can stay at the top, too.

I can state that no matter how reckless we may have been in our personal lives at times, we never cheated anyone or pulled a fast one when someone wasn't looking. In New York City, you couldn't possibly survive in the nightclub business for nearly thirty years if you were always cutting corners—especially with the police, fire, and building departments, the IRS, lawyers, staff, security, talent, or any of the hundreds of people and departments and agencies that could and would trip you up.

Lots of the nightclubs that were our competition at one time or another were toppled by problems with greedy owners' taxes or lawsuits or similar issues. Limelight, Tunnel USA, Studio 54, Twilo, Sound Factory (and the list goes on) were closed and many of their owners went to prison for the corners they cut and the laws they dodged. Some of the old and shuttered clubs were turned into apartment buildings or college dorms. We ran Webster Hall for more then twenty-five years without a scandal. Being selected by the public, bands, managers, and road crews as the best nightclub and music venue in the world by the prestigious *Pollstar* in 2017 was a nice gift from the industry to us—and one we earned.

Our family succeeded at Webster Hall because of our vision, passion, hard work, and our ability to follow the rules of both life and business. We found the right location, dreamed up creative ideas for promotion (both inside and outside of the club), booked the right entertainment, and made sure everyone was safe and had a good time. In the next few pages, I'm going to show you some ways we ensured our success and give you some advice to help you follow in our footsteps and avoid potential pitfalls.

To be successful in the nightclub business, or any business for that matter, you should:

- Start with a good idea;

- Find a good location;
- Work hard;
- Pour all of your passion into your business;
- Start on a good financial footing; and
- Maintain financial clarity.

But the absolute most important step to success in business is this one:

Treat all people well.

In the following pages, I discuss some specific areas that are important in any business enterprise, especially the nightclub scene. These next few sections are presented in alphabetical order, but be sure to read the last one: Staffing. It's the most important one of all.

AUTHORITIES: BUILD A GOOD RELATIONSHIP WITH MUNICIPAL AND COMMUNITY FOLKS

We learned early in our careers that the police do not want to deal with arguments, fights, or other disorders in entertainment establishments, and they also don't want the neighbors making lots of complaints about noise or crowds. The police will respect you and listen to your side of any situation if you can prove you know how to run security for your business and don't need to ask them to get involved very often.

After the 2015 massacre in Paris where terrorists killed almost 130 people in the Bataclan theater, the NYPD asked all public assembly building owners and operators to meet for a discussion on public safety. The police spokesman that day told the audience they should all run their public assembly buildings and businesses like Webster Hall does. That was certainly nice to hear.

Here are some tricks for cultivating a good relationship with the police and other authorities:

- Listen closely, especially to the police and your neighbors. Don't talk much; listen. Only talk when asked a question and only answer that question. Don't volunteer information unless you are asked.
- Stop any potential trouble at the front door. You are serving booze

and fun inside your club, so you are responsible for anyone you let in your front door.

- Don't skimp on security, even when money is tight.

Every night we had a small army of at least forty men and women at the front door and throughout the club, enforcing our policies. You couldn't enter if you were drunk, loud, abrasive, or a big group of single men. Everyone was frisked for guns and drugs. We did not let noisy or badly behaved patrons into our club. The front doors were the only place we could take full control of customers' behavior. Once they were let inside, any bad behavior they caused was our responsibility.

We turned away potential troublemakers and escorted out clients who could not meet our standards of good behavior. Our strict standards weren't always met with kindness. The ones who cursed us out for monitoring their bad behavior or excessive foul language would read us the riot act from top to bottom and would eventually have to be sent home or be escorted to safety from themselves.

However, 99.9 percent of our guests behaved beautifully. They waited their turn to get in and allowed us to frisk them while being extremely polite and cordial to our security and service staff. In our twenty-five years of full operations, we could count on two hands the number of physical fights we had to deal with, which is pretty mind-blowing when you consider we hosted 3,000 people a night from all over the world.

That required our amazing attitudes and training—and the brave souls who guarded our front doors and kept our patrons safe. A great example was our sweet, loyal and fair friend, Blondie, who was buried in a Webster Hall Security shirt, supporting us all the way to her grave.

THE SECRET TO BUSINESS LONGEVITY: ACCOUNTABILITY AND PROFESSIONALISM

Lots of NYC nightclubs only lasted a few years, and quite a few of their owners and operators wound up in prison. How did we survive so long?

I'm not about to gloat, but the secret to our success can be summed up in two words: accountability and professionalism.

Webster Hall was a huge nightclub located smack dab in the middle of thousands of apartments, which meant we had constant dealings with the police (local, municipal, and federal) as well as the area fire departments and building inspectors and more. Having a liquor license in New York State is a privilege, not a right, and we had to continually prove that we deserved that privilege.

We had thirty-seven licenses to operate Webster Hall all coming needing to be renewed at various times every year: furnace inspection, health inspection, air contracts, food and liquor handlers license—the list goes on and on. You could not forget about any one of them, so we had a full-time lawyer who maintained all thirty-seven licenses and their annual renewals. When a city "march" department (police, health, fire, building, immigration, and employment officials) entered into a full-to-the-rafters nightclub in the heart of the East Village unannounced at midnight on a Saturday night, you better have all of those licenses in order.

We never brought in any black-market liquor or beer to sell for un-taxed dollars , so when the authorities checked our liquor closets, all of our products were accounted for. We also checked every patron's ID before and frisked them thoroughly before we let them in the door, so we could always be accountable as to who was in our club at any given time and know they were not armed.

For our first ten years, you had to be over twenty-one old to enter. One night Leonardo DiCaprio came by with an entourage. It wasn't his first visit, and he had enjoyed previous times at Webster Hall. But this night Bijou Philips was with his group. She was still a teenager and we would not let her in. As a result, Leo left, and his crew left with him. We never wanted to turn away celebrities, but we did not bend our rules for them either.

GIVE RESPECT; EARN RESPECT

We also never missed a monthly police precinct council meeting in over twenty-eight years because we knew the captain would be giving the local community updates on any crime or issues. We sat in that crowd quietly and listened for any complaints regarding Webster Hall so we could defend ourselves as the police referred the complaint to us. We also attended the meetings to show the police we respected their time.

We made sure to never attempt to engage in any bribes with the authorities. Instead, we respected them and paid our fines without complaints.

Two weeks before the sale of Webster Hall, the police invited me down to Police Headquarters with no explanation. I was obviously nervous when I was greeted by a group of distinguished, white-shirted police who proceeded to show me exactly how they ran New York City— from the facial recognition technology department to the big room that pinpoints every police officer's location. It blew me away. People should know what a great, clever, and proactive police force New York City has.

Then they told me they knew I would be leaving Webster Hall soon and wanted to thank me for how well we Ballingers had run the massive nightclub for so many years . They said the police had experienced far less trouble with us during our time at Webster Hall years than they did with so many of the smaller clubs that ran their clubs by the seat of their pants.

BRANDING: GROW YOUR IMAGE AND PROFIT FROM IT

Learn to curate, activate, compensate, and plan the brand for your business. Understand that the glamour and the glitz of a Webster Hall or a Big Bop or any well-created business brand are built on the foundation of repeatedly doing very well the small things that made the business successful in the first place.

How do you know when to make additions to your business or subtract old ideas that are showing signs of wear and tear?

First, keep your eyes on your weekly attendance (or the customer engagement equivalent for your business) since it is always your most important clue. If your attendance slips more than three weeks in a row, immediately activate the promotion team and have them reach out to your targeted audience with discounts or other features that will give your clients immediate gratification.

At Webster Hall, that would be free drinks and/or free admission before midnight to draw a crowd that makes the location look super busy. People love people and FOMO (fear of missing out) is most everybody's biggest motivator.

BE INNOVATIVE. AND ALSO CONSISTENT.

Your most important business tool is consistency. People get used to your business style and don't really like to see it change. So whenever you make a change, focus on improving the small things first. The old saying, "Look after your pennies and your dollars will take care of themselves," is true. Another truthful old saying is "The customer is always right." If you want to be successful, be respectful, diligent, and keep your mouth shut unless your opinions are asked for.

Create fun new promotions that echo your original successful promotions. For example, we hosted amazing gay-centric parties every week for nearly forty years. We embraced all sorts of ideologies. We always knew in gay circles that the "Bears" (older working men and dad-types with plaid shirts, big tummies, and bigger beards) loved the "Twinks" (young, slender, effeminate types) and the Twinks loved the Bears. So we created specific events tailored just for these two groups. We also knew the "Leather and Lace" types (more masculine lesbians) and the more feminine "Fems" adored each other, so we followed their lead and created customized parties they would enjoy.

Because of our years of work, we created value in the very name of Webster Hall. We created this value because of our reputation and the way we ran our business. This was our brand and it proved quite profitable when it came time to sell our club. We worked hard to maintain the brand we had built and in the end it paid off.

CUSTOMER SERVICE: TAKE CARE OF THE LITTLE GUYS

The most important people in our business were the little guys. The ones who stood in the rain for two hours with their girlfriends and boyfriends and let us search them without complaining. Let us charge them thirty dollars each and then went home and told everyone it was the greatest night of their lives. We were always smart enough to know that the celebrities and rich people expected everything for free and left you as soon as the next hot spot opened.

So, we came up with a well-deserved perk we could give to the little guys who came to the club and behaved themselves. A "Webster Hall Membership Card" would allow them to come back for free before midnight on any night we were open and not having a special event or big-time concert. These club memberships were valid for life. So when tourists and first-timers came to our clubs, they would see a huge crowd already inside dancing, drinking, flirting, and looking like they owned the place. Webster Hall looked like a place you wanted to be.

We knew many of our membership cardholders on a first-name basis. A lot of them came adorned in costume like Phantom of the Opera, or their favorite musicians. They would climb onto the raised platforms we had strategically placed around our dance floor and become cheerleaders for the entire club.

THE GREATEST OF THESE IS LOVE

In Webster Hall, you were among friends. No matter what your station was in your everyday life, you were one of us here. And we were all equal under a canopy of music, mayhem, love, laughter, and dancing.

Our formula was simple, easy to understand, and inclusive. We kept all our dance floors bumping to different genres of dance music—rock 'n' roll, Latina, hip-hop, house, salsa. You name it, we played it. Celebrities would be dancing with taxi drivers and bodega owners. Nannies would be pulling Wall Street power players around the dance floor by their noses.

The most important key to our success was love. My brothers and I loved our clubs so much that we sent that vibe out into the universe. And because we respected our own place of business, the staff and customers followed suit and respected each other.

INVENTORY CONTROLS: TRUST AND INVENTORY ARE UNEXPECTEDLY CONNECTED

Your stock and inventory systems play a surprisingly important role in your team's morale—while also serving as terrific economic measurements. Always assume your staff is correctly handling your inventory rather than assuming they are shortchanging your business. Learn to reward your staff for their basic honesty instead of making them feel as if they are constantly under suspicion.

Stick to the most basic inventory controls that allow you to reconcile how much you paid for your products and calculate how many dollars you grossed on those products each month. Then calculate the percentage of costs versus income.

This simple rule, when followed diligently, will give you the true answers. Using this simple inventory method will allow you to save money by not investing in technology you may not need. You will also make your staff feel trusted.

Yes, there will sometimes be theft, giveaways, and waste, but if you follow this simple method you will quickly know when your point-of-sale staff are slacking—or worse. This approach also takes a lot of stress off yourself, management, and staff.

When we operated Webster Hall, our only question for the accounting department was, "How many people came last night?" A good nightclub operator judges his business on attendance, as well as revenue. Myself and others in the business had a long-standing joke about who had the longest late-night line waiting to get in. That person (in our minds) was the coolest operator because we knew a lineup is a nightclub's best friend. With late lines comes consistency.

Luckily, Webster Hall had the most amazing account manager named Theron Mirabelle. He started with us as a part-time accountant for our small but successful Webster Hall record label. When we were forced to pull back on the label, Theron moved into the office to help with our new live music format. When we started booking 3,000 bands a year, all needing deposits and reconciliations, our business changed dramatically. Theron balanced a huge payroll, made all the talent payouts, managed our insurance, and kept up with too many other duties to mention.

I still don't know how Theron was able to manage a nightclub grossing $25 million annually, pay 170 staff members, and balance payouts for all the talent we booked. He was also involved with the actual sale of Webster Hall, which as you can imagine, was a world of change in and of itself. Wherever you are now, Theron, thank you, my friend.

We had another accountant who had fallen asleep at the wheel and seldom came into the office. But he was associated with the landlord. They say keep your friends close and your enemies closer, so I kept him on board and paid his wage until the day we left.

LAWYERS: KEEP AN EYE ON THEM

Watch the lawyers closely; they are not your friends, and you can't always trust them. They only care about money, so never mistake their concern about you or your legal issues because the only thing they really care about is how much money you have and how much they can make.

I feel the firm I hired to close the sale of Webster Hall cost us more than a million and a half dollars to basically transfer a lease because they were in no rush to close the deal. Monitor invoices from lawyers and law firms closely. Question their fees all the time—too many of them care only about their fees. A bad lawyer can make your case drag on for years. A good lawyer makes it last even longer.

LEGAL AND ACCOUNTING: DEFICIENCIES AND EFFICIENCIES

Never claim expenses that might raise a red flag for your business. Audits happen when the auditor notices odd little things that others just take for granted. I learned to take no expense deductions so that we wouldn't trigger a red flag. Also, don't file for tax extensions. Get your taxes in on time to show you are honest, organized, and professional.

The single biggest challenge of running a nightclub and music venue with an annual income of $20 million was, of course, the money. Fortunately, one of my personal strengths was that I was incredibly good with numbers. I could look at a full house and tell you how many people were in the building, and my estimate would either be spot on or off by only a few people. I could also estimate off the top of my head how many dollars we would gross that night and come within $200 of the total. The only two questions I ever asked our awesome staff and night managers were, "How many people came last night?" and "Did everyone have fun?"

Balancing a budget for a business that financial institutions did not like to deal with was always my top priority. We had a staff of 170 full- and part time employees and a $1.5 million monthly payroll and operating cost, but we didn't own our building so could not provide the necessary collateral for a line of credit. During all of this, we were met with nights that really tested our strength, such as the few times when the authorities closed us down to prevent overcrowding or to investigate a crime or suspected crime.

When something like that happened, I would be left scampering to find enough funds to meet payroll and pay rent, liability insurance, and a million other expenses. But for all our challenges, we never missed a payroll, or a month's rent, or an insurance payment. And we made money for ourselves every year for forty years we were in business.

We could always call a vendor or supplier if we needed an extra week or two to pay their bill. Our big holiday events—such as our New Year's Eve parties and our one-of-a-kind Halloween events—could make up for lean months and allow us to bring any semi-delinquent accounts up to date.

Although money was always challenging, I could never let anyone know that because so many predatory types were always lurking. Promoters, for one, would take any money problems as a sign of weakness. We always had to appear calm, cool, collected, and in charge.

Of course, I never had a lot of personal funds to put away. But complaining about money would have been a losing game. Nearly everyone on our staff lived paycheck to paycheck, so getting them paid on time was very important to me, and I honestly believe the majority of our wonderful staff knew that.

DON'T BORROW FROM THE IRS

In 2009, after banking with Chase for nearly 20 years, I asked for a loan to make some in-house changes. Our rent had tripled that year after what I considered shady dealing from The Bowery Presents, and I was happy when the bank agreed to the loan. I went ahead with the changes expecting the $500,000 loan, which we now refer to as "the loan that never came." That left us in a really tight spot, but we were able to dodge a bullet, thanks to our patience and a new young team, when our EDM format took off.

We also ran into some big trouble with the IRS when I decided to withhold the required sales tax remittance to pay for the club's renovations. The six months I withheld the remittance became the most expensive loan I would ever get. The IRS makes the *Soprano's* collection techniques look like the Red Cross. They were relentless and constantly threatened to close us down.

Thankfully, my good friend and lawyer—yes a lawyer—Richard Pawelcyk was able to negotiate a payback schedule, which we were able to meet, barely. The measly $600,000 remittance we withheld wound up costing us nearly $1.2 million with penalties and interest. One lesson we learned from this episode: never mess around with the IRS.

Money was always tight between ghost wages and no-show jobs. Meeting our $150,000 weekly payroll was brutal, but we met it every week—although sometimes without a dollar to spare.

My advice for businesses in similar situations:

- Take money management seriously. Find people who are extremely frugal by nature and very good with numbers to care for this side of your business.
- Always come clean to the people that matter and they will work with you.
- Don't let the predators know about any money issues. They will stalk you, start rumors about you, and hope you close so they can pounce on your assets.
- Include respect, concern, and a workable solution for money problems or debts of your suppliers and other business partners.
- Pay your employees well and on time.
- Never mess around with the IRS.

MAINTENANCE, INSURANCE, AND TAXES

"Lon, you've got to get down here right away! The cops are here with firefighters, and they've closed the place up!" Murray shouted into the phone.

It was 10:00 on a Saturday night. A night not unlike all the past years of Saturday nights at Webster Hall. Only this time, there was real panic in Murray's voice. During a concert featuring the thrash metal band New Found Glory, a woman on the first floor attending our wildly successful off-Broadway, interactive musical saw the ceiling and lights bouncing back and forth from the level above. She panicked and called the fire department.

It was 2003, and everyone in New York was more on edge about building collapses since the 9/11 attacks. The fire chief who responded was new in the position, and when he saw the ceiling warping in and out, he stopped everything and ordered everyone in the place, all 2,000 of them, to vacate immediately.

I left my family and guests to drive to the club as soon as Murray called. When I arrived, I saw my brothers talking with the police and fire authorities. We stayed quiet and listened respectfully to what the firefighters were saying, which was the Ballinger style. It was not good news.

By then local news channels were saying the roof at Webster Hall had caved in and people were still inside and that they were waiting on reports of fatalities. The New York press loves drama and blood—even if they have to make it up.

Fortunately, New York City has extremely sophisticated and experienced people in the Building Department, and the leading engineer was helping us. This young man calmly took Steve, Buster, and me aside to give us his briefing.

We were relieved to find out the engineer was a native New Yorker whose father had owned a restaurant and bar in Queens, so he understood that our livelihoods and the livelihoods of many others relied on this old building. We explained that Webster Hall had been built as a public assembly building over 120 years earlier, that the entire building was wrapped in iron girders, and that each floor and balcony famously moved up and down—on purpose. It was designed this way because the nineteenth-century engineers knew that a building designed to host live music, large crowds, and aggressive dancing would need give so it would not crack and break.

This clever engineer told us, "I'm closing you guys up for the night. I believe what you're telling me, but these are crazy times, and we'll have to prove to the fire department, politicians and the public, that we've followed protocol."

My brothers and I put our heads together to try to determine how we could prove that the floors in Webster Hall were meant to sway— safely. With some advice from our old friend Mark Mina, we called in a volunteer fire department from a local Long Island town and rented 200 three-thousand-pound boxes we could line across the main floor. We filled each container with two tons of water—water that came from the outside fire hydrants—and we had the 200 tanks filled with 400 tons of water had placed on the big dance floor. And guess what? The dance floor didn't move a hair. The New York City building department gave us the green light to reopen just in time for our next scheduled event. The moral of this story is the age- old saying: Where there's a will, there's always a way. Or man made the problem so man can fix the problem . . . thanks for that one, Dad.

Fire was always a worry when we were squeezing 3,000 people into a 150-year-old building with narrow stairwells and limited exits. One night in 2008, my son Tom and a very diligent security guard saved Webster Hall from a huge fire disaster. That night, we had only one small act playing in our 400-person basement studio, which we frequently did during the early days of the week. On those nights, the security guards would walk throughout the building looking for people who might have gotten lost or intentionally found their way to the closed floors. After one walkthrough, the security guard told Tom he smelled smoke in the Grand Ballroom. Tom went up to investigate and noticed a small flame flickering through the acoustic ceiling tile.

With no time to waste, he grabbed a portable fire extinguisher, dragged it up a ladder at the back of the stage, and climbed into the ceiling, where he found the motor for an air handler on fire. He was able to stall the flames but not extinguish them. By the time the fire department arrived, Tom had dragged three more fire extinguishers into the ceiling to take on the fire. If he hadn't been there to battle it, the entire roof would have exploded within ten minutes.

The firemen sent the arson team to investigate the fire and concluded it was a mechanical disfunction.

NEIGHBORS: BE GOOD ONES

When it came to community relations, we always took the high road and worked to find compromises. For example, when a neighbor would complain about the noise coming from Webster Hall, we often offered to buy them an air conditioner to mask the sound. We bought a lot of air conditioners, and they were worth every penny because they bought us lots of goodwill.

When we first arrived in New York, the streets in front of and around Webster Hall were filthy. We not only cleaned up those streets, we kept them clean every year we were there.

Webster Hall had every legal right to be where it was and to conduct its business the way it wanted, so we could have dealt with neighbor complaints with a heavy hand, but we truly believe that nice guys finish first. So we did all we could to win others over with kindness and respect.

Did it always work? Not always, but most times it defused a difficult situation, and there was no bad blood between us and the community. Every once in a while no matter what we tried, our approach didn't have the desired effect. One unhappy person who happened to work for the city tore up the sidewalk in front of the club.

I firmly believe that to create a culture of positivity I must never take away another person's dignity. So, if you have problems to be solved, get the person alone so they can save face. Also, never get personal, which will almost always cause the other person to get defensive. Today, more than ever, be very careful with what you say to others.

Let actions speak louder than words.

We would host the neighbors for steak dinners and breakfast buffets, and they were always allowed in to the club for free before midnight. They were able to see the best shows at no charge and never had to pay for a drink.

One neighbor in particular was a community activist who saw us as wild guys and wanted us to leave. We explained (nicely) that was never going to happen. But we showed her we were responsible family men who wanted to improve the neighborhood. I brought my wife and kids to meet her and the other neighbors and promised her we were nothing like previous operators. It didn't happen overnight, but we won over most of the neighbors and co-existed peacefully for many years.

PROMOTIONS: FILL THE HOUSE WITH HAPPY CUSTOMERS

As a hospitality and entertainment business owner/operator, promotions are the way you get people interested in your club and eager to visit you for the first time—or again and again. Events, merchandise, or theme nights can often be the difference between positive cash flow or negative cash flow.

Theme nights helped us keep our clubs booked on Wednesday nights, which meant a weekend blizzard that kept the crowds at home would not wreck our business. In Toronto, at The Big Bop, we created a Wednesday night promotion called Depression Wednesday with all drinks for $2.50. Our radio ads would scream, "Bust the piggy bank, pick up the change and head on over for Depression Wednesday."

Overall, our club promotions were usually very basic, such as a major discount on admission or drinks until a specific hour. Or a little show we concocted, such as a big dunk tank. You can read more about our overall strategies for promoting Webster Hall in the chapter, "Marketing and Promoting For Success."

When you're in the nightclub business for forty years, you're going to create some memorable and effective promotions. (Sometimes the memorable ones were also the effective ones!) In the next few pages, I want to describe some specific promotions we created in hopes that you can find some ideas for your own business. Pick and choose from our ideas, but don't go overboard in any business venture unless you feel very confident in your own ability to market your own ideas in your own way.

AERIAL PERFORMERS

Starting with our very first club on the side of Grand River in Cambridge, Ontario, we sought out daredevil circus acts: high-wire walkers, flying trapeze acts, and beautiful women in skimpy little outfits doing what is called the cloud swing. They would use a big rope looped from the ceiling and simply twirl and dance leaving their audiences spellbound.

Ian Garden was the quintessential godfather of Canadian circus acts. He had been a performer, an elephant poop cleaner, and ultimately, the owner of the legendary Garden Brothers Circus. He was fascinated by our willingness to showcase and pay for what at the time were the best circus acts in the world. From the Horton Brothers Skating Bears playing hockey on the club's gigantic gazebo to the Wallenda family's motorcycle acts buzzing around in a large metal ball. He told me how he had created promotions to being extra people into his famous circus shows and said you have to get people inside, even if that meant putting a gun to their head and a $5 bill in their pocket.

Garden told me a lesson he had learned from working for the Vargas family circus. If Mr. Vargas saw a bunch of young people standing outside the tent, he would ask why they weren't going to the circus. If they said they didn't have enough money for tickets, he would ask, "Well, how much do you have?"

They might say, "Fifty cents!"

So he would lead them to the back of the tent, lift up the flap, and let them in for free. When someone asked why, Vargas would say, "Well, they have fifty cents and they're going to spend it on my popcorn."

AUCTIONS

We created what we called "singles auctions" for both women and men. An auctioneer on a small stage would "sell" an individual, and then that person and the buyer would get two free drink tickets each and a chance to sit together (chaperoned) for up to thirty minutes to see if they wanted to continue the "date." It was all for fun and it worked. (It was different times, for sure, and it probably couldn't be done today.) We also created a dating site in our club where you could post your name and who you were looking to meet on a monitored chalkboard and what time you would be at the board, ready to meet. This proved to be a big promotional hit.

CONTESTS

We had amateur burlesque contests for both men and women. Tipsy Tim Bauman, a Webster Hall record executive who became a legendary lawyer, would host the contest and the winner would get a $500 cash prize. This Friday night special consistently drew 3,000 people who paid big door fees to get a birds-eye view of the male and female exhibitionists who all fought to get selected for the contest. Just for the record, nobody was pressured to do anything they didn't want to do.

CUSTOMERS–WOMEN

As I have discussed in other places in this book, we always knew that women were our most valuable customers. We catered to women, treated them with respect, and made them feel safe in our club. We always had a Ladies Night at every club—always. Women got in free on Ladies Night and ruled the roost from the moment we opened until the minute we closed.

CUSTOMERS–YOUTH

It's hard to be everything for everyone. We came close, but we also knew that it was easier to market our venues when we aimed for a specific target. So our promotions often targeted young people because we knew they were the group that would go anywhere, anytime, for a chance to meet someone new. In other words, in hopes of getting laid. We knew that clubs were really opportunities for young people to meet the love of their lives, and many did just that in our venues.

CUSTOMERS–AVERAGE JOES

When Webster Hall became incredibly popular, we began attracting the rich and famous. But our bread-and-butter promotions were always aimed at the average Joes of the world. For many reasons they were our ideal customer and the foundation for all of our clubs.

EMAIL LISTS

We recognized the power of the internet early and began selling tickets online. In that process, we also gathered buyers' email addresses, creating a mailing list that eventually grew to a whopping one million Webster Hall members. These email lists became the marketing backbone of our music business, allowing us to advertise without having to purchase television, radio, or print ads. The worm had turned. Where once we begged radio stations like Z-100 for marketing handouts, they eventually were begging us for show tickets and event sponsorships.

JOHN AND JIM

We often hired street people to "stand guard" somewhere innocuous or to wear our Webster Hall T-shirts through the neighborhood. We never questioned their skill level or their sobriety. But our willingness to pay for their services meant we could always count on their support if something bad went down on the street like a fight or a theft. John and Jim were twin brothers who were war veterans but also alcoholics who lived on the East Village Streets in the early days of Webster Hall. John and Jim would make sure our mom made it home safely after she worked until the wee hours of the morning. Sometimes that just meant following Mom and her security guard to her apartment building across the street, but we took care of John and Jim because they took care of her.

Good businesspeople should look for ways to make things better for others. It can gain you as much attention as a good promotion and also buy you goodwill for your business. Better yet, it's the right thing to do for the good of all humanity.

MEMBER LOYALTY CARDS

Our membership cards were always our most popular promotions. They allowed free admission before midnight, and you could get membership cards when you bought a ticket for our New Year's Eve bash. We also used them to reward our loyal customers and to placate our neighbors. The loyalty cards helped create a community and helped fill our club with happy people before the hard-partying late-night customers arrived.

NUTS AND BOLTS

We offered nuts-and-bolts parties. Men would get bolts of varying sizes when they entered the club and the women would get different sizes of nuts. Then you tried to match your bolt with a nut or vice versa. When you found a correct match, you could redeem the nut and bolt at the bar for free drinks. And hey, you never know what could happen next!

RADIO AND TELEVISION

Word-of-mouth marketing was always our best method, but we also promoted ourselves via radio and sometimes television. A well-created radio ad allowed us to say exactly what we thought our customers would like to hear. We told people who we were and what we offered them. We never cared if critics approved of our ads or not. Though we were always treated well by the press, we learned not to count on them but created our own ads where we could control our own messages.

REFERRALS

We used the human connection to keep our business successful. When a taxi would pull up to one of our clubs, a designated front-door person would give the taxi driver a $5 bill and thank him kindly for dropping off paying customers. The taxi driver would earn a little extra money and then be quick to recommend our club to future passengers. We would often see the same taxi driver several times in a night.

SPECIAL EVENTS

"Five thousand dollars? Oh my God, I was going to drop out of school. I can't believe I won this money," a young, overwhelmed NYU student told us as we counted out fifty $100 bills as his reward for winning one of our Halloween contests. We owned Halloween—to the point we called it "Halloweek." From our original Ballinger's in Cambridge to the legendary Webster Hall, Halloween was our big night, our Super Bowl if you will.

We offered huge cash prizes for the best costumes and would select twelve or fifteen from some of the most incredible costumes the human mind could imagine. It wasn't always the most expensive costume that would win. Instead, it was the costume that made the crowd laugh the hardest.

Like the one year a flaccid penis made from rubber came flopping onto the big stage in the Grand Ballroom and then grew big and hard as the human inside the costume started pumping it with air. After he had achieved a full erection, he used another pump to spray the entire crowd with water. The crowd howled with laughter, and there was no need to wait for a winner to be announced. The big dick walked home that night $5,000 richer and the crowd left laughing. Using the crowds to entertain each other was one way we cast our magic spell.

We would also create a gay Halloween and/or a Halloween party for the service industry. We were always the official afterparty for the incredible NYC Halloween parade, so we could get four Halloween celebration nights in one week. This helped us create an income flow that could carry us through winter weekends when nasty weather could cut our paying crowds in half.

We pulled every trick in the book out of our back pockets on the big nights like Halloween, New Year's Eve, Valentine's Day, Saint Patrick's Day, and Cinco de Mayo. At Webster Hall, all were marked with celebrations and over-the-top events.

"STREET WALKERS"

We would pay our jugglers, magicians, stilt walkers, and other entertainers a little extra to go to busy tourist areas and hand out passes that
allowed free entrance to Webster Hall before midnight. This technique
drew big crowds of onlookers and helped keep our club packed earlier
in the night. We knew that tourists wanted to see a full booming house
of happy revelers when they arrived. And we also knew that the be-
fore-midnight pass holders usually went home early while the cash-pay-
ing tourists liked to come late and stay late.

SIGNS

We embraced guerilla marketing techniques that could—but seldom
did—lead to a small fine or a finger-wagging warning from the cops.
For example, we might create a hand-painted poster on big white drop
sheet. Then we would send a couple of people to unfurl the sheet on a
big bridge over a busy highway during morning rush hour. In a couple
of hours tens of thousands of motorists would discover that Webster
Hall was hosting a huge party that night. Of course, we would leave the
moment the authorities told us to.

SOCIAL MEDIA

"Dad," my son Tom said, "You have to try to remember that anybody
who writes terrible things about others on social media platforms have
no friends and nobody really likes them." This advice helped me keep
my eyes on the real value of the new social media platforms and helped
me to mitigate the frustration I felt when someone wrote a horrible re-
view for the whole world to see. I had to remind myself that these harsh
reviews and vitriol usually said more about the writer's own character
than it did about their perceived grievances with us.

So, instead of worrying about Yelp reviews, I started putting more
value and effort to become the most "Tweeted" music venue in the
entire world. In 2015, we had 144,000 tweets originating from our venue, which more than offset a few bad Yelp reviews. (Note: Around that
time, we joined a class-action lawsuit against Yelp for asking for money

to remove nasty reviews. The lawsuit forced Yelp to drop its pay-for-play rules.)

TRENDS

Marketing has changed dramatically since we first started in business in 1979. It was more hands-on then, and there were no Yelp reviews to worry about. Still, your best tool remains the same—word of mouth.

We embraced the gay community and the hip-hop community and the EDM community and other groups that were marginalized elsewhere. They all came to Webster Hall and then they came back and brought their friends who came back and brought their friends.

Running our own promotions kept us close to our customers and made it easier to spot the trends that invariably pop up in this business. We always catered to young people, and their attention spans are notoriously short and their tastes and preferences can turn on a dime. One of the most important parts of promoting our business was always doing our best to stay relevant.

SECURITY: PROTECT YOUR PLACE, YOUR STAFF, AND YOUR CUSTOMERS

It surprises people when I tell them Webster Hall was never robbed. I'm sure some people thought about it, but we had such good security that they thought twice, and decided against it. Exceptional security was the cornerstone of our success at Webster Hall.

From the beginning, we knew we could create a New York City icon with Webster Hall, and we knew just how to do it. We would be a club that represented all the cultures of the city. No one was going to be any more special than the person waiting in line behind them. Our only real rule would be that everyone must behave themselves. We maintained that philosophy from the day we opened until the day we left.

We did our best to never allow weapons or drugs into Webster Hall by physically searching every would-be customer who wanted to enter our building. It didn't matter if they were a celebrity, an FBI agent, or an off-duty NYPD officer. A gun owner could keep their bullets, but we took their guns and kept them in a gun safe in the main office. We placed the weapons in a numbered bag and gave the gun owner a matching number so he could reclaim it at the end of the night—just like a coat check.

Our approach proved to be a smart strategy because one Saturday night we confiscated forty pistols. Soon enough, Webster Hall became known as a no-carry zone and our clients fell in line. The ones who didn't want to comply with our rules could hang out elsewhere. We didn't want weapons, drugs, or bad attitudes in our club.

FIRM, FAIR, KIND

We ran security like the best police forces run their precincts. We were firm, fair, and kind. We wanted the police to know we were running a safe business because that's the way you make friends with the police.

Our security personnel included highly skilled professionals with EMT training and experience in our unique type of business. We expected our security workers to show respect while keeping order in a crowded, high-volume, pressure-packed environment that relies on alcohol and people in high spirits in order to stay sustainable. They learned to never take clients' comments, frustrations or anger, personally and to enforce our rules with all.

Our front-door policies were always serious and stringent; talking back or making a scene would get you barred for the night. We knew anyone who was rude to our front-door staff would be a handful inside the club, especially after downing a few drinks. Our heavy-handed entry policies won the respect of our staff, the police, and—most important—the women. And they came to Webster Hall in droves because they felt safe there.

If you are running a nightclub or similar business, know that the "keepers of the gate" are vitally important to your success. Our first line of defense was always made up of a group of formidable men and women dressed in black. Many were former police officers with permits to carry guns and getting one over on them was next to impossible. They were smart, professional, and efficient.

Security personnel (and the busboys) were always the first to know what was really going on and whether it was good or bad. A good security person can see trouble a mile away. Our security was the very best in the world, and we watched them perform selflessly night after night. There was a reason they called themselves, "The Webster Family."

STAFFING: CLUB MANAGEMENT IS PEOPLE MANAGEMENT

Emotionally intelligent people often become business leaders even though they are not always the smartest or most talented people on the team. But they know how to listen to everyone's point of view, never take the glory for themselves, and always insist that great work is being done by everyone else.

Your best employees are the same. They're the ones you never hear about. They do great work with no fuss and they never leave any messes behind. They don't have to be told what to do; they simply take the initiative and do what needs to be done.

In the club business, there is one more aspect to staffing that is important: the staff should never become the entertainment. That means the staff at a nightclub has to behave. We all make our living at this club, and we don't want to see it ruined by misbehaving employees.

We didn't expect our Webster Hall employees to be angels, but we had did have guidelines and rules we expected them to follow. One of those was no using or selling drugs (or at the very least, don't get caught) at work. The New York Police Department often had undercover agents inside Webster Hall, and they would have shut us down if they caught an employee selling drugs.

We expected and wanted our staff to have fun as well as work hard, but they had to keep their hands—and any stupid talk—to themselves. Everyone who walked through our doors was now one of us, and our goal was to make sure everyone enjoyed their journey through the nightlife in a safe way. Arguably even more importantly, we knew our entire livelihoods depended on us keeping our liquor license in good standing. We lasted for thirty years by not allowing our staff to go (too) crazy.

A FAMILY ATMOSPHERE

We hired a diverse group of people to serve in key positions because diversity is the straw that stirs the drinks of cultural prosperity. Our nightclubs were so successful because we didn't discriminate against anyone. We treated our staff fairly and expected them to treat all our customers with the same kind of respect.

We also wanted the people who worked for us to feel like a part of the family. A good example of this vibe was J.P., a brilliant man who was not able to hold a "regular" job after he fell out of a third-story window and spent months in a coma. In the twenty-seven years he worked at Webster Hall, J.P. did every kind of odd job—he swept the street, took out the trash, and broke down boxes. At the end of each night, J.P. would clean up every piece of garbage outside—whether it belonged to us or not. He left the streets around Webster Hall as clean as a whistle, so our neighbors wouldn't be able to accuse us of being slobs. He was so proud of his job, loved the work, and was fiercely loyal. Hiring people like J.P. served us well. Their longevity and loyalty created a warm and cozy atmosphere that was hard to explain, but you could feel it.

We often said we didn't own Webster Hall; it belonged to New York City and its people. In the same way, we also wanted our staff to take ownership of their jobs. Unlike some other clubs, we paid our people by check instead of in cash, so it was set up like a regular job—not a nightclub-specific one where cash was king and your salary might depend on how many people came in the doors on a given evening. We gave our people a lot of responsibility, allowed them do a lot of different jobs, and made sure they learned a lot when working for us.

When a staff member leaves, no matter what position the person held, ask yourself, why did they leave? Where did they go after they left? What could we have done differently to either keep a good employee or avoid hiring another less-than-stellar one? Hiring, training, paying, and trusting an employee is a big investment in time and money. The last thing you want to do is lose a valuable, long-term employee. If your business consistently has high staff turnover, then you're likely headed for trouble.

LEAD BY EXAMPLE

It isn't easy to keep morale and spirits up when you're dealing with a nomadic group like hospitality and entertainment workers. Making your staff feel valued and creating a work environment where they want to stay (and not just for the money) is the goal. You do that by respecting everyone. Try to not pick favorites. Listen to their problems and concerns like they are your problems—because in a way they are—and do your best to accommodate any personal and home/life issues that arise. I guess what I'm saying is you should treat employees like family—that is if you respect, appreciate, and want a relationship with *your* family.

I believe that it's better to show people how to do their job versus just telling them how to do it and explaining what is expected. I like to lead by example. If I show up on time, work hard, act responsibly, do the right thing in the right way, don't complain, and keep my cool under pressure, my staff is more likely to do the same. My secret in managing people is to never lose control, to seek compromise when possible, to stay positive, and to make sure everyone is happy whenever possible. I never felt the need to get revenge; I believe in karma.

And of course, pay your people promptly and fairly. In the end, people work for a paycheck. Let them share in your success. Give them a bonus when appropriate and offer other perks and incentives that matter to your employees. Even things that seem small to you are appreciated.

I have discovered you don't have to be rich to be happy, but you have to be happy to be rich. I loved my "job," and I would like to think the people around me picked up on my joy and tried to find joy in their work as well.

LOOK FOR MOTIVATION

If you are a small independent business, then always try to hire people who have a passion for your product—even if that means you wind up picking a more enthusiastic person over a more experienced candidate. You can't give people passion for a project—they must have it in their souls.

Create a sense of healthy competition in your creative team where efforts to support a promotion or launch a new enterprise can be recognized as both individual accomplishments and a team victory. Assign tasks to specific employees and then have weekly meetings where you follow up gently and positively to discuss results. After all, you are the private sector and small businesses can only survive with proven results.

PAY SPECIAL ATTENTION TO YOUR MANAGEMENT TEAM

You must treat your management employees like your special family members. These are the ones who enforce the owners' will. The ones who make your business goals work. They work many hours and do all the dirty work like staff discipline and deal with emergencies and work late every night so you can go home and have dinner with your family and friends.

When they screw up, cut them some slack—unless their misdeed falls in sexual or theft categories. Then you have to act immediately. When you're dealing with the law or possible lawsuits, it's never really about what happened—it's more about what happened when you found out about what happened.

You must understand that in the eyes of the law, you will seldom be found guilty or be criticized if you react to accusations correctly. If you find out about a business or staff-related incident and follow all the rules and the letter of the law, you won't be judged unfairly. Show concern, immediately contact the proper authorities, and activate all avenues of retribution.

PARTNER WITH YOUR GENERAL STAFF

For thirty years we ran a 170-member staff, including coat check, security, washroom attendants, porters, bartenders, waiters, go-go dancers, and managers at many levels—all under intense workloads.

And in thirty years, we never had a staff member sue us for anything—including sexual harassment or other employee issues. Why? Because they were our partners, each and every one, who received a paycheck from us at the same time every week. They were our trusted partners in every way.

When we hired anyone for any position, we gave them a Webster Hall employee handbook clearly stating our expectations from them. The handbook also spelled out clear rules on what to do if they felt they were being intimidated or mistreated in any way. We also allowed our employees to think and act like the adults they were.

We seldom lost staff, and over sixty stayed with us for our entire run in New York City, even if they only worked for the special holidays or a few days a month to help them catch up on a few bills. Your staff is your backbone, and they represent your business to the public. So be good to your working and creative staff and it will pay you back time after time.

Some people only viewed Webster Hall as a rundown hedonistic venue. Their opinions were superficial, and I think even lazy (like Bob Dylan's song, "Lay Lady Lay," our club was worn, but our hands were clean). All four floors were cleaned and washed every day we were open. We embraced our building's history no matter how worn out it may have looked to outsiders.

And we also cleaned up every piece of garbage around our big club—a job that was maintained by the legendary J. P., our first employee. For twenty-five years, J. P. cleaned the four-block radius around our club every day at 4:00 a.m. We wanted to prove to our neighbors we believed in cleanliness and we paid attention to the details. You never smelled stale beer, cigarettes, urine, dirt, or vomit. Never. We had the most loyal cleaning staff who worked endlessly to keep our club fresh and clean.

THE IMPORTANCE OF DIGNITY

Always leave a person with their dignity in place. I think this is one of the most important lessons for any young businessperson to remember, whether you are dealing with employees, or customers, or suppliers, or competitors.

You don't have to always have the last word. And a kind word (or three) can go a long way to making someone feel good about themselves. I've mentioned this before in this book. I just had to say it again. That's how important I think it is.

ONE LAST THING

Here's another little thing I learned that actually makes a big impact. Always do your very best to learn the first names of all your employees and anyone who has any business with you at any level. Use first names whenever possible. This immediately paints you in a positive light, ingratiating you into their thoughts with goodwill.

On the other hand, if you are dealing with a superior or anyone who holds any kind of influence over you, use a courtesy title and their last name (Mr. Jones, Mrs. Smith, Dr. Who) unless they tell you to do otherwise.

WEBSTER HALL HISTORICAL FACTS

- Webster Hall was built in 1886 as a place for entertainment, banquets, weddings, conventions, and meetings of all kinds.
- In the early years, Webster Hall was known as a meeting place for liberal-leaning political activities. It often served as a meeting place for people who wanted social change that benefitted everyone.
- Webster Hall became famous in the early twentieth century for hosting masquerade balls with skimpy and outrageous costumes (for the times) and attracted the Bohemians of the Village. The Ballingers' Webster Hall became known for similar parties and events in the early days of the twenty-first century.
- Prohibition didn't stop the party, and Webster Hall became a well-known speakeasy in the 1920s—also called the "Jazz Age." Al Capone was said to own a portion of the club, which was known then as "The Devil's Playhouse."
- In the 1920s, gay and lesbian groups were allowed to host events and parties without interference from the police or politicians.

These groups called Webster Hall "The People's Stage," because it was known as welcoming anyone and everyone regardless of race or sexual preference.

- Over the years the hall burned to the ground and was rebuilt four times.

- In the late 1950s, RCA turned the space into Webster Hall Studios. Frank Sinatra, Elvis Presley, Julie Andrews, and many other famous artists all recorded there. Soundtracks to films such as *Hello Dolly!, South Pacific,* and *Fiddler on the Roof* were also recorded there.

- In 1980, Webster Hall became The Ritz nightclub, which hosted live performances by Tina Turner, U2, Sting, Guns 'N Roses, and others. Rows of subwoofers and stacks of speakers allowed The Ritz to have a large sound for its size.

- In 1992, the Ballinger Brothers arrived from Canada and took over the building and a new game was on. The venue was re-renamed Webster Hall, and it became known as New York City's Club.

- For the next twenty-five years the Ballingers ran the most profound, eclectic, and truly diversified 3,000-person nightclub in the history of America. Everyone was welcome to enjoy four floors of culturally accessible music and a genuine cast of characters who held the city in awe with their warm and inviting mayhem of fun, dancing, trapeze acts, and high-wire walkers. Superstar musicians and other artists all clamored to play or just join the fun.

- The Ballingers sold Webster Hall to a music conglomerate in 2017.

- Webster Hall was closed for months of renovation but reopened in 2019 and remains a successful New York City music hall today.

Bonus Section 2

PHOTOS THROUGH THE DECADES

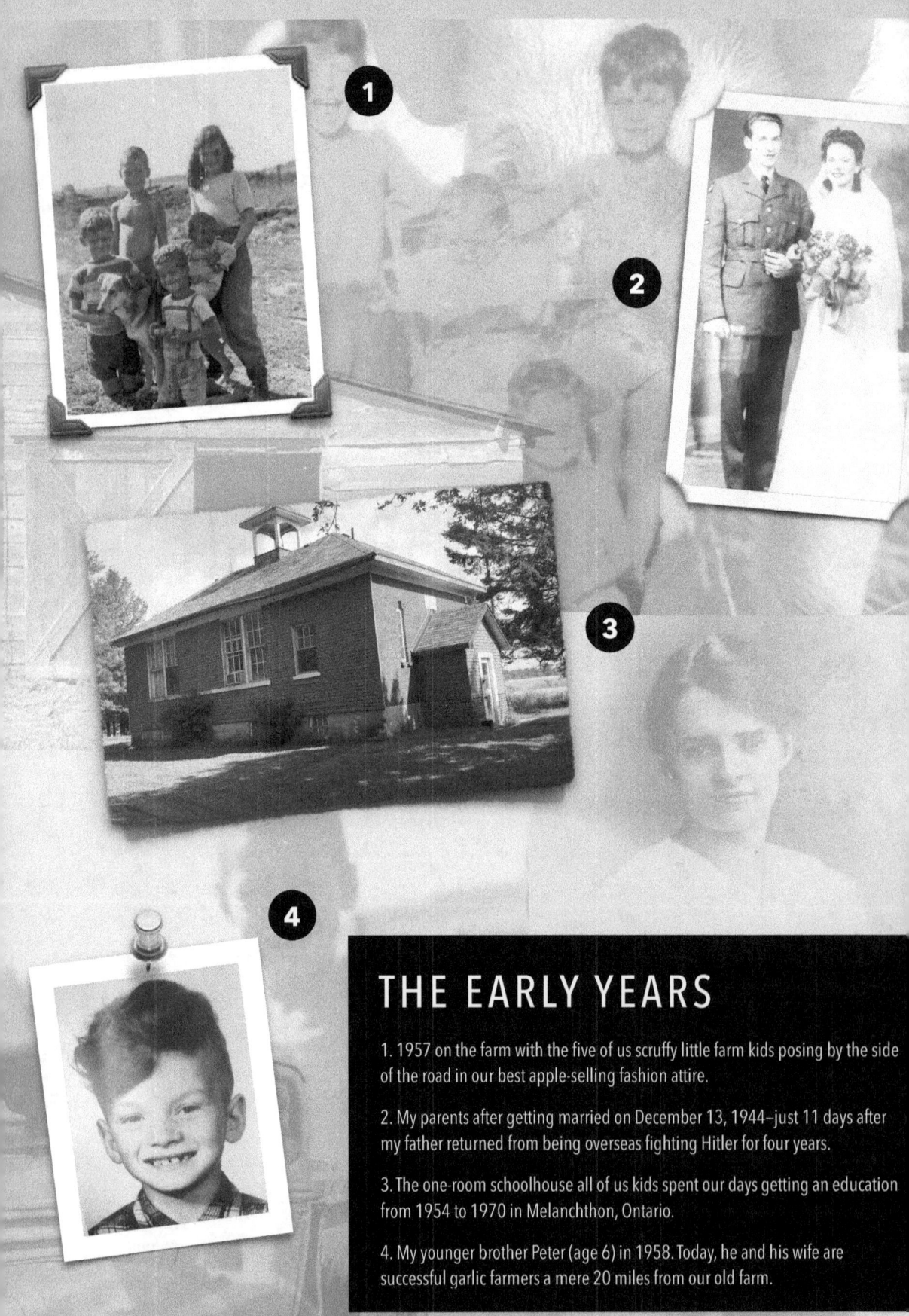

THE EARLY YEARS

1. 1957 on the farm with the five of us scruffy little farm kids posing by the side of the road in our best apple-selling fashion attire.

2. My parents after getting married on December 13, 1944–just 11 days after my father returned from being overseas fighting Hitler for four years.

3. The one-room schoolhouse all of us kids spent our days getting an education from 1954 to 1970 in Melanchthon, Ontario.

4. My younger brother Peter (age 6) in 1958. Today, he and his wife are successful garlic farmers a mere 20 miles from our old farm.

THE CANADA YEARS

1. The Ballinger's always knew how to throw a party–a house party in 1988.

2. The Big Bop in 1986, 6151 Queen Street West in Toronto.

3. My brothers and I being interviewed for an in-depth piece on CBC in 1989.

4. The Highlands Badminton Club in 1946, long before it became Ballinger's.

5. Our former Dundalk smoke shop and laundromat as it looks today.

6. The auction notice for our old farm, March 21, 1974.

THE CANADA YEARS

1. The boys planning to open a pizza parlor in 1972.

2. The Big Bop in 2000 hits the skids after we left for New York.

3. The *Toronto Globe* on our booming Canadian club businesses in 1983.

4. A typical Big Bop office meeting in 1988.

5. Legendary Big Bop DJ Avery doing his thing.

6. Dancing the night away in 1989.

THE BALLINGERS

1. The Ballinger family (minus Dad) all grown up in 2006.

2. Jon Vreeland, my cousin and Vice President of Webster Hall Records.

3. Lon and Lois Ballinger posing at The River Grill near their new venture, The Stewart House, in Athens, New York in 2020.

4. President Clinton in 1996 accepting a keepsake gift from Mrs. B, Steve, and Buster (not shown) as he boards Air Force One at LaGuardia Airport.

5. My daughter Rachel enjoying life in 2005.

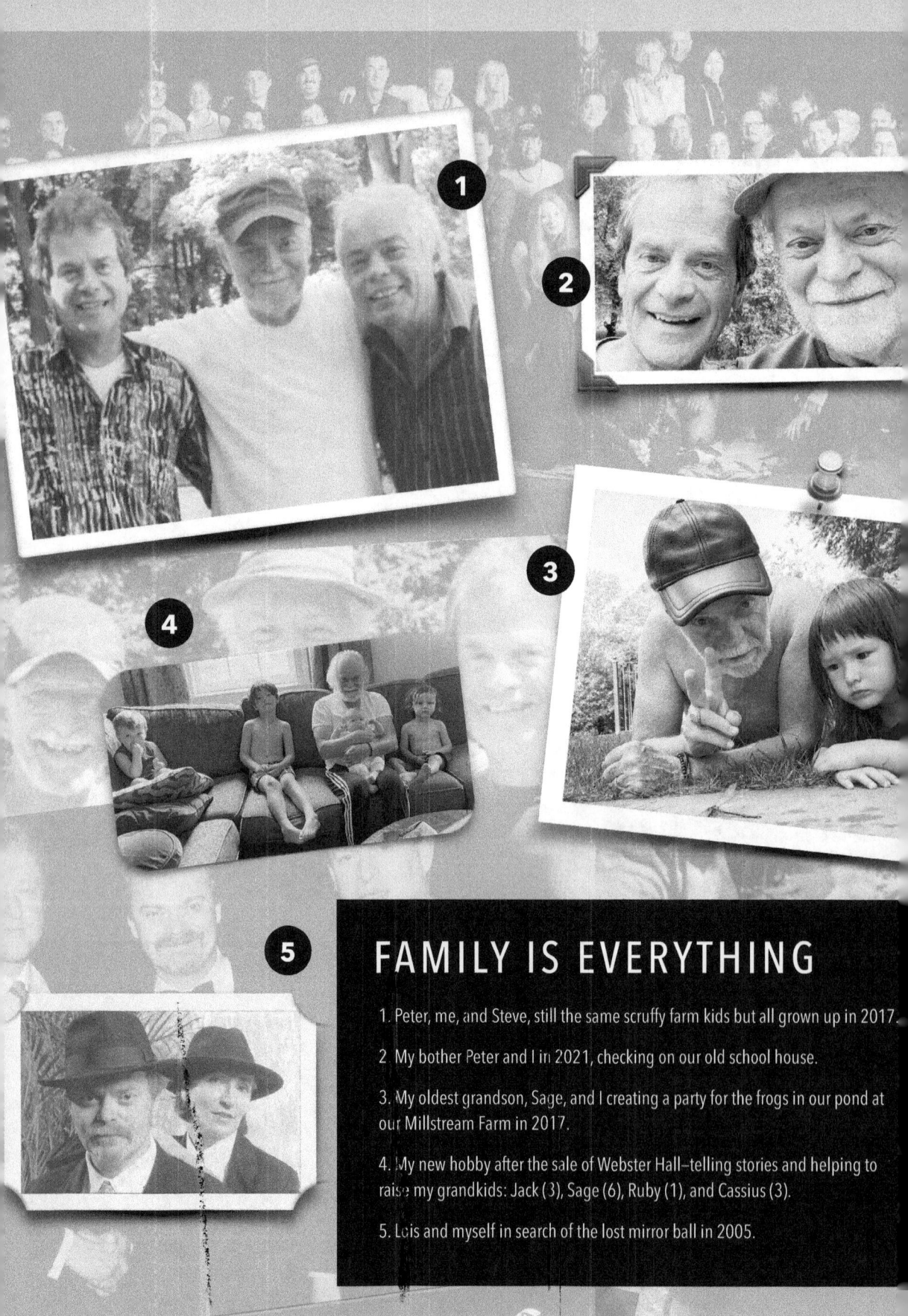

FAMILY IS EVERYTHING

1. Peter, me, and Steve, still the same scruffy farm kids but all grown up in 2017.

2. My bother Peter and I in 2021, checking on our old school house.

3. My oldest grandson, Sage, and I creating a party for the frogs in our pond at our Millstream Farm in 2017.

4. My new hobby after the sale of Webster Hall—telling stories and helping to raise my grandkids: Jack (3), Sage (6), Ruby (1), and Cassius (3).

5. Lois and myself in search of the lost mirror ball in 2005.

THE POWER OF FAMILY

1. "The Original Five," our nickname when we left Canada for New York in 2004.

2. Our family celebrating 20 years in the USA in 2015.

3. Gail, "The Elder" Ballinger, embracing her little brother (me) in 2009.

4. The Steve Ballinger family meeting Bill Clinton at Webster Hall in 1996.

5. Celebrating the life of Mrs. B in 2015. Pictured is a collection of Ballinger fathers and sons posed as "The Ten Handsome Men of Webster Hall."

THE NEW YORK YEARS

1. Legendary Tito, the trapeze artist who sadly fell to his death one day.

2. Me and my good pal, Manhattan District Attorney Robert Morgantheau.

3. The sign proves our commitment to embracing the future of digital in 2015.

4. Our studio club considered the best 300-seat music club in America.

5. From farm boys to old men, the brothers (minus Buster) in 2017.

6. Elle King and mom celebrating her 2013 show in our 300-seat studio.

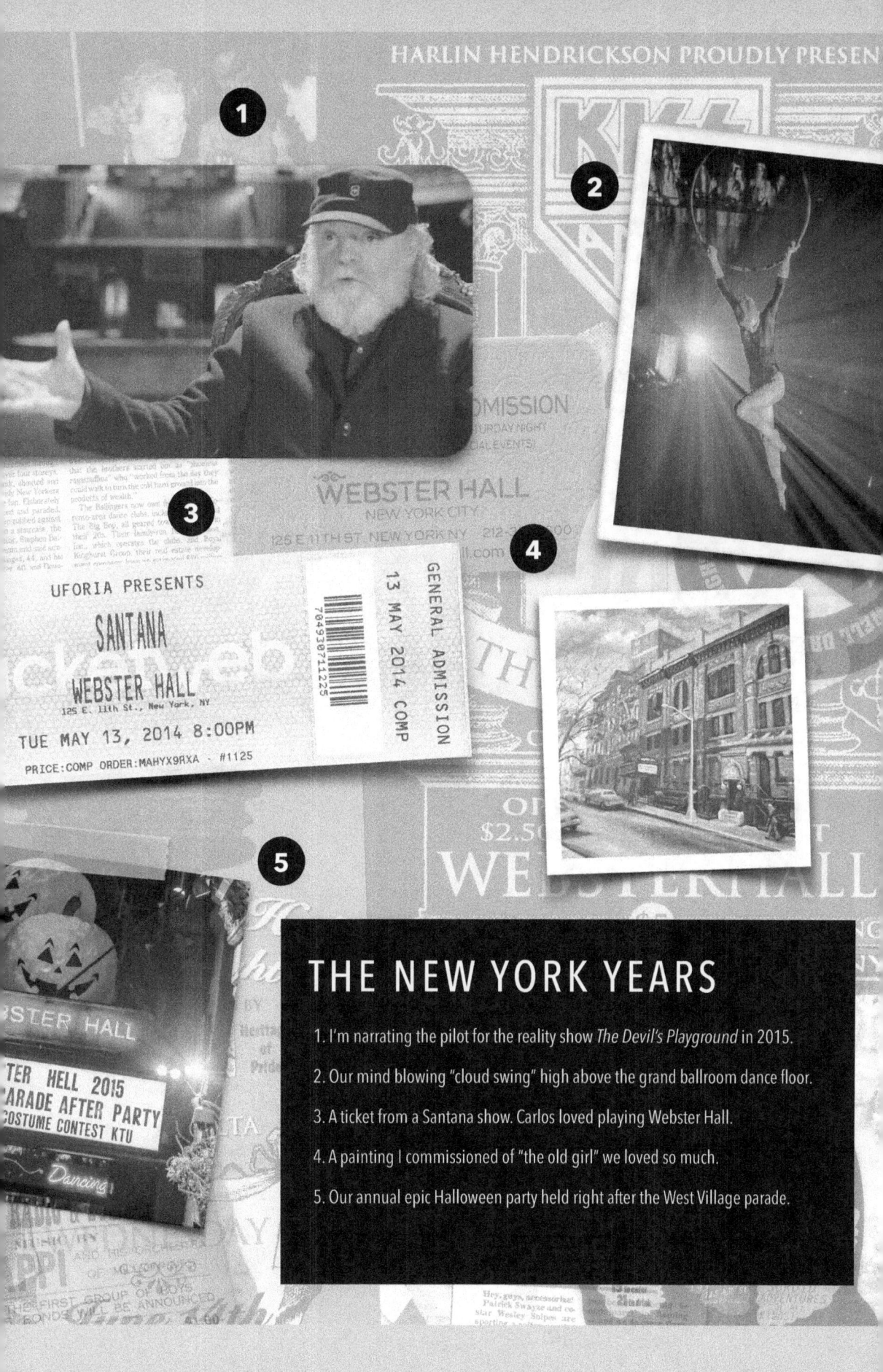

THE NEW YORK YEARS

1. I'm narrating the pilot for the reality show *The Devil's Playground* in 2015.

2. Our mind blowing "cloud swing" high above the grand ballroom dance floor.

3. A ticket from a Santana show. Carlos loved playing Webster Hall.

4. A painting I commissioned of "the old girl" we loved so much.

5. Our annual epic Halloween party held right after the West Village parade.

THE NEW YORK YEARS

1. My tearful goodbye speech to the staff on our very last night.

2. Kim and Kanye bringing bedlam and chaos to Webster Hall in 2016, which was handled expertly by extraordinary security team.

3. Part of our eye-popping stage show for the 2009 MLB All-Star Game.

4. A crowd shot of our grand ballroom and bar, capturing a typical night.

5. Richard Pawelczyk, our longtime lawyer and forever friend.

THE NEW YORK YEARS

1. Ed Sheeran sharing his extraordinary talents in our tiny studio in 2015.

2. The illustrious Mrs. B, guarding her flock until she was 95 years old.

3. L-R Top Row: Kenny, Nicolas, Blaise, Rachel, Lon, Tom, Stephen, Jr, and Gray.

3. L-R Bottom Row: Adam, Eric, Kaelin, Lois, and Christina–The Ballingers.

4. Flyer for our legendary night Hip Hop party held on a Thursday, the night ladies were always welcomed in for free.

WEBSTER HALL

THE END OF AN ERA

THE NEW YORK YEARS

1. Lois and I in 2017 saying thank you and goodbye to New York City after nearly 30 years at the top of the heap.

2. I am forever grateful to Gerard McNamee, Jr., who was there for us.

3. Trent Reznor of Nine Inch Nails always loved the Webster Hall vibe.

4. Webster Hall Records in 1997 achieved "Indy Gold" with our NY Dance CD.

5. Lois Ballinger bravely judging the Biggest Buns contest.

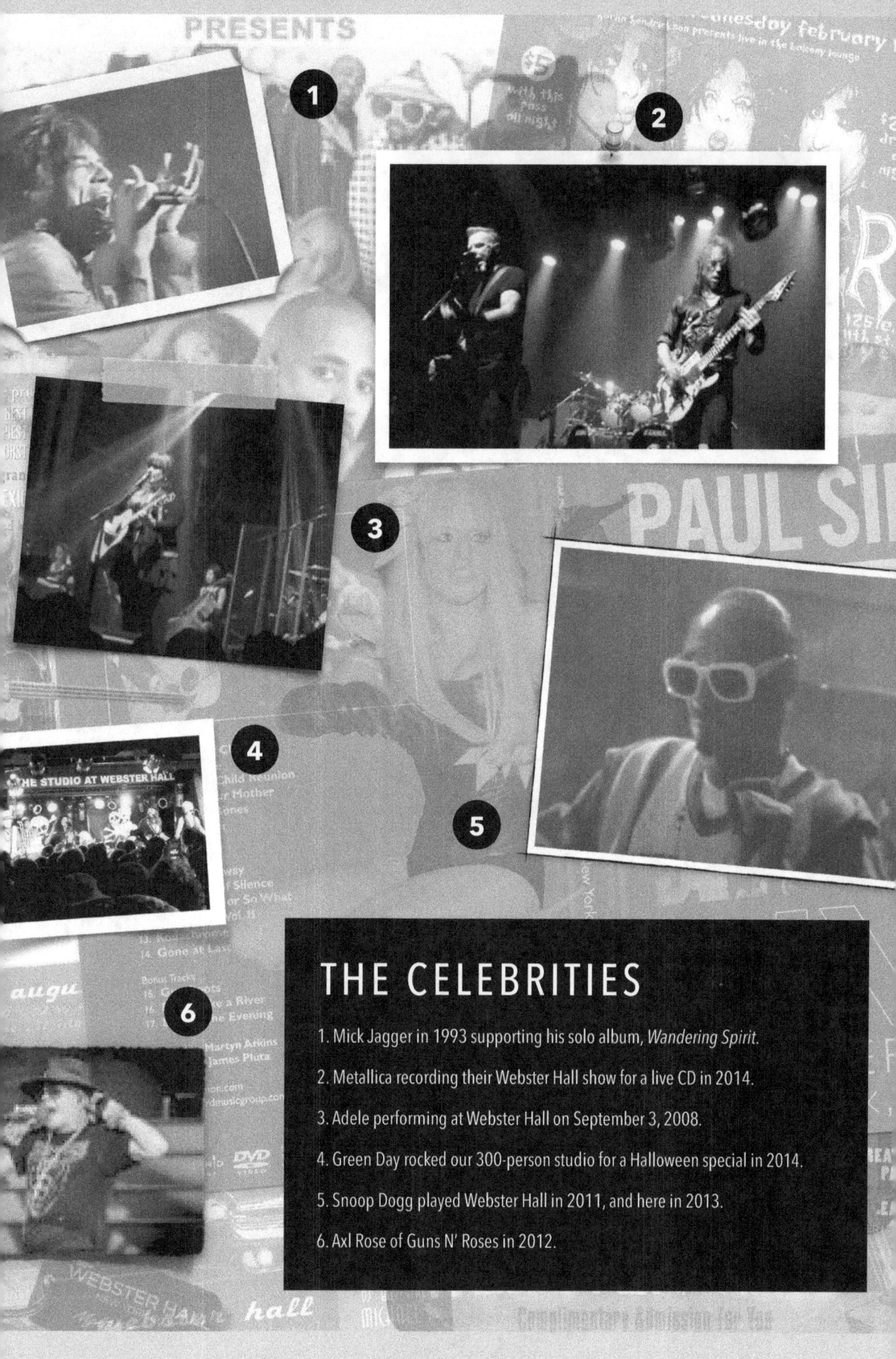

THE CELEBRITIES

1. Mick Jagger in 1993 supporting his solo album, *Wandering Spirit*.

2. Metallica recording their Webster Hall show for a live CD in 2014.

3. Adele performing at Webster Hall on September 3, 2008.

4. Green Day rocked our 300-person studio for a Halloween special in 2014.

5. Snoop Dogg played Webster Hall in 2011, and here in 2013.

6. Axl Rose of Guns N' Roses in 2012.

THE CELEBRITIES

1. Tom Ballinger and 50 Cent performing at Webster Hall in June of 2014.

2. That's me on the Giant's sideline with Eli Manning in 2011.

3. Madonna's "Pajama Party" in 1995 promoting her album, *Bedtime Stories*.

4. Prince's performance at Webster Hall in 2005 was one for the ages.

5. Tom Jones backstage at Webster Hall with Mrs. B (my mom) in 1994.

6. Keith Urban performs in 2009.

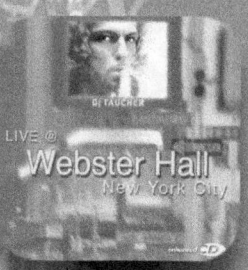

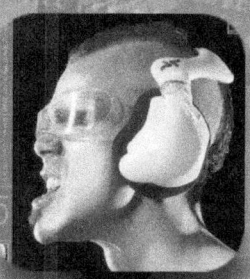

WEBSTER HALL RECORDS

EARLY CREATORS OF EDM: 1996-2003

We took the unique dance mixes from the four huge dance floors of Webster Hall and packaged them as CDs—which went on to sell millions upon millions of copies and lead us into the new millennium laughing and dancing all the way. May the beat go on.

To listen to these mixes for free go to: PartyBoysNewYork.com

A Track

Cosmic Gate

Zedd

The Bloody Beet Root

Masterkraft

Skrillex

THE SUPERSTAR DJ ERA

THE DJ YEARS: 1997-2017

Just like we recognized the power of the early hip hop artistry of The Cold Crush Brothers, Busta Rhymes, and Grandmaster Flash, we also helped to create the birth of the superstar DJ—from an early Deadmaus to a young Avicci, Tiesto, and Skrillex. In fact, there were so many amazing DJs we put them on our big stage where they became legitimate big league superstars.

To listen to some of their mixes for free go to: PartyBoysNewYork.com

1

2

3

4

5

6

THE BEAT GOES ON

1. Come visit us at the historical Stewart House in Athens, New York.

2. The City Beer Hall is located in downtown Albany, New York.

3. The C.B.H's cozy craft beer bar, with DJs and dancing upstairs on weekends.

4. The Seneca Bar and Cafe, located in the heart of Ridgewood Queens has the best burgers… guaranteed.

5. Meet us in the historic bar at the 1833 Stewart House.

6. The Mud Club in Woodstock, New York.

AUTHOR'S NOTE

First, I would like to thank my wife, Lois. Without her support and cool head for the last fifty-two years, we might never have survived. My brothers, Steve, Peter, and Buster; my sister, Gail; and my mom and dad were on the team every step of the way. I would also like to thank my children, Kaelin, Rachel, and Tom, who were always there to help and support me. To all our many friends and nephews and nieces, thank you.

To our many wonderful staff members, your hard work, stylish demeanor, and loyalty meant so much to our success.

I would like to thank: Lee Silber for his beginning-to-end creative spirit and positive energy and his amazing literary and graphic skills. Glen Edelstein for his wisdom and great connections; Marla Markman for her intelligent and intuitive direction; Tammy Ditmore for her really great editing services; Andrew Chapman for his skillful quarterbacking with the book design plus his graphic work; Simon Burnstall for his photography contributions; and a big thank-you to Frank Enea and Satellite recording studios in Mount Kisco, New York for the audio recording.

To anyone else who contributed to this book that I may have inadvertently overlooked, thank you. You were not forgotten on purpose. This book is not so much about me as it is about us. I appreciate everyone who contributed in one way or another to our success. .

And last but not least, to all of the millions upon millions of customers who supported our vision for the nearly thirty years as we remained the top nightclub and music venue in the greatest city on earth . . . thank you. Because it never would have worked without your support.

ABOUT THE AUTHOR

Lon Ballinger and his brothers created and operated the most successful nightclubs in Canada and built more than 300,000 square feet of downtown Toronto commercial space from 1978 to 1994. Lon and his brothers then transitioned to New York City where they built Webster Hall into the world's most successful entertainment venue of its size. In twenty-five years, they hosted over thirty million patrons across four floors of distinct programming. In a groundbreaking cross-promotional initiative, Lon Ballinger founded Webster Hall Records, which sold over two million recordings while creating the original footprint for the worldwide electronic dance music phenomenon. Since selling Webster Hall, the Ballinger brothers have all gravitated to the historic and exploding-with-newfound-passions Hudson Valley, where they run a series of successful new hospitality business ventures. Visit PartyBoysNewYork.com for more details.

THANK YOU!

Thank you for reading our story. It truly was a unique and exciting journey for us. Our next big adventure takes place in the exciting Hudson Valley region, a historical destination—the birth place of America—full of vibrant new opportunities for us and so many others.

See for yourself why we have chosen the spectacular Catskills Mountain range for our family's future endeavors. The many famous villages and towns come together with a new generation of people we are helping to claw back our important American history with new-found prosperities.

Join us in the Hudson Valley at all of the new businesses that my family and other entrepreneurs just like us are creating and bringing to life.

Long live America, the greatest country on this earth.

For more details, please check us out at (and maybe tell your own nightclub story) at PartyBoysNewYork.com.

—Lon